"In *Rescuing Ambition*, Dave Harvey distinguishes ambition for the glory of God, which is good, from ambition for the glory of self, which is bad. But godly ambition doesn't exist in a ʌ̵꞊ ꞊ ꞊ ꞊ ꞊ ꞊ ꞊ ꞊ Harvey helps us see how it is intertwined with humility, contentment, faith, a Dave Harvey is both an experienced pastor and a gifted writer, so you will profitable but also hard to put down."

    JERRY BRIDGES, author, *The Pursuit of Holiness*

"Thomas Watson said, 'Selfish ambition is the mother of all schisms.' But Dᵢ better way in *Rescuing Ambition*. With wit and wisdom, Dave uncovers the tru how God forms a gospel-driven ambition in us for use in his mission and for leader in the church today will read *Rescuing Ambition*."

    ED STETZER, President, LifeWay Research

"Dave Harvey thinks well, writes well, tells good stories, and cites people of s I have long appreciated Dave's integrity, wisdom and perspective. Were I not ambition for greatness, or my ambition to write a memorable endorsement, I wou *Ambition* is biblical, honest, witty, and sometimes amusing. I'm happy to recom on an important and overlooked subject."

    RANDY ALCORN, author, *If God is Good* and *Heaven*

"*Rescuing Ambition* is a book for all of us who were created by God, who strive to excel. It applies to every Christian. Dave Harvey brilliantly and accessibly answers the question, 'Can Christians be humble and ambitious at the same time?' He explains why and how we can, always rooting his presentation in Scripture. This is a book that has needed to be written. You will not be disappointed."

    JIM TEBBE, Vice President of Missions; Director, Urbana Missions Conference, Intervarsity Christian Fellowship

"Whether you're on Main Street or Wall Street this book has something to say to you. No author has done a better job of helping me understand my heart, my motives, and my Savior. Harvey uses humor, Scripture, and real-life examples to help us balance our dreams and callings, while always reminding us that Jesus is the Christ."

    JOSH DECKARD, Former Assistant Press Secretary to President Bush

"I've always been a pretty ambitious person. I don't like ceilings or limits. I love thinking and dreaming about doing great things, about being a part of something great, something world-changing—and I've always felt guilty about this. I've wrestled with my motives and why I want to do great things. My struggle has been how to discern the difference in my own heart between selfish ambition and a God-centered drive in life. And to err on the safe side, I have at times tended to reduce the size of my dreams and lower my expectations. Under the banner of trying to be humble, I settle for less. I suppose I'll struggle with this tension for the rest of my fallen life in this broken world, but, thanks to Dave Harvey, I now have a new tool in my toolbox to help me sort through these things in a gospel-drenched way. Thank you Dave!"

    TULLIAN TCHIVIDJIAN, Pastor, Coral Ridge Presbyterian Church, Fort Lauderdale, Florida; author, *Unfashionable: Making a Difference in the World by Being Different*

"Ambition is war; a battle between the sin-driven pursuit of autonomy, self-sufficiency, and self-glory and a humble desire that everything you do would reflect the one thing that is excellent in every way, the glory of God. On every page, Harvey alerts us to this war and trains us to be good soldiers."

    PAUL TRIPP, President, Paul Tripp Ministries

"As the leader of an organization expressly dedicated to seeing the gospel deepen in our own lives as well as expand outward to the nations, I'm grateful for Dave Harvey's recovery of the idea of ambition. Dave's book is a powerful, plainspoken, Scripture-saturated reminder that when the gospel is the center of our identity and security, we can be freed from the petty dreams and small-minded motivations that often hamstring ministry. In the gospel, we find the freedom to be truly ambitious."

    BOB OSBORNE, Executive Director, World Harvest Mission

"From page one, Dave's writing style gripped me with his humor, humility, and down-to-earth, Bible-saturated style. I don't think I have ever seen a book on ambition, but I have been trying to provoke men to find some ambition, borrow some, or if they were really ambitious, even steal some! Dave writes to those of us who aren't ambitious enough to read (much less comprehend) a thick theological treatise, but are interested enough to read the words of someone who understands that we are often content to watch others with ambition as they ride up mountains, compose great music, and attempt the unthinkable—like homeschool three kids. This is not a self-help book that doesn't really help; it is a wake-up alarm to rouse the good gifts specifically placed within us by God for his own glory."

SCOTT THOMAS, Director, Acts 29 Church Planting Network

"I didn't know that my ambition was defective and in need of rescuing until I read this book. Harvey writes with such compelling insight and clarity that you're left thinking the lack of godly ambition ranks alongside pragmatism and theological flimsiness as ailments afflicting the church today. Yet, at root, this book isn't about problem-hunting nearly as much as it is about the gospel, salvation, and embracing the ambitious agenda Jesus sets for our lives. Those who want to live with high and glorious purpose for the Savior must read this book. So do those who don't, and those who never thought about what godly ambition really involves. *Rescuing Ambition* calls us to live large, bold lives by swiping as much glory for Jesus as possible."

THABITI ANYABWILE, Senior Pastor, First Baptist Church of Grand Cayman; author, *The Faithful Preacher*

"Dave Harvey teaches us that God wants ambition back in our understanding of godliness and spiritual health. As Christians, we are to be zealous for good works (Titus 2:13)—that is, ambitious for them. We are to be people who dream and do big things for the glory of God and the good of others. Let's not be content with small dreams cloaked in a guise of humility. This is a critical book for the church today because it helps us recover the spirit of William Carey, who ambitiously said 'Expect great things from God. Attempt great things for God.'"

MATT PERMAN, Director of Strategy, Desiring God Ministries

"Dave Harvey has delivered a compelling case for developing God-ward ambition in the lives of men and women alike. This insightful book carries a timely message in our 'whatever' culture: we all have ambition, but where it is aimed and how it is used is worth serious consideration. With self-effacing humor, Dave reveals how being wired for glory can either corrupt us or lead us to a divine agenda. Highly recommended!"

CAROLYN MCCULLEY, author, *Radical Womanhood: Feminine Faith in a Feminist World* and *Did I Kiss Marriage Goodbye? Trusting God with a Hope Deferred*

"Only an ambitious person would try to rescue ambition! Only an ambitious person would actually take the time to write a book on the topic. And only a humble person could accomplish the task! There is a vast difference between selfish ambition and godly ambition. If you want to know what sets them apart, read this book and discover the radical difference between self-glory and God's glory. As in his book on marriage, *When Sinners Say "I Do,"* you will find Dave writing out of his own failures and growth in grace. Interestingly, ambition can be rescued but you won't get there without bathing ambition in gospel virtues and life experiences like humility, service, contentment, failure, and community. And you won't get there without a Redeemer. Dave makes certain that you meet this Redeemer, Jesus, throughout the pages of this book. If you struggle with selfish ambition or lack ambition altogether, this book will help you."

TIMOTHY S. LANE, Executive Director and Faculty, Christian Counseling and Educational Foundation

"Dave Harvey isn't satisfied to live a mediocre life and he isn't satisfied to see the followers of Jesus live that way either. In his down-to-earth style, Dave takes the concept of ambition from the 'reject' pile of Christian vocabulary and reminds us that it is desirable, no, it is a gospel imperative to be ambitious for the right reasons and the right goals. His arguments are not psycho-babble, either, but grounded in scripture, theologically sound, and intensely practical."

TIM WITMER, Professor of Practical Theology, Westminster Theological Seminary

Rescuing
Ambition

Dave Harvey

FOREWORD BY C. J. MAHANEY

⠿ CROSSWAY

WHEATON, ILLINOIS

Cover design: Josh Dennis

Cover photo: David Sacks

First printing 2010

Printed in the United States of America

Unless otherwise indicated, Scripture quotations are from the ESV® Bible (*The Holy Bible, English Standard Version®*), copyright © 2001 by Crossway. Used by permission. All rights reserved.

Scripture quotations marked KJV are from the *King James Version* of the Bible.

Scripture references marked NIV are from *The Holy Bible: New International Version®*. Copyright © 1973, 1978, 1984 Biblica. Used by permission of Zondervan. All rights reserved. The "NIV" and "New International Version" trademarks are registered in the United States Patent and Trademark Office by Biblica. Use of either trademark requires the permission of Biblica.

All emphases in Scripture quotations have been added by the author.

ISBN-13: 978-1-4335-1491-3
ISBN-10: 1-4335-1491-5
PDF ISBN: 978-1-4335-1492-0
Mobipocket ISBN: 978-1-4335-1493-7
ePub ISBN: 978-1-4335-2356-4

Library of Congress Cataloging-in-Publication Data
Harvey, David T. (David Thomas), 1960–
   Rescuing ambition / Dave Harvey ; foreword by C. J. Mahaney.
      p. cm.
   Includes bibliographical references.
   ISBN 13: 978-1-4335-1491-3 (tpb)
   ISBN 10: 1-4335-1491-5 (tpb)
   ISBN 13: 978-1-4335-1492-0 (hbk)
   ISBN 13: 978-1-4335-1493-7 (mobipocket)
   1. Success—Religious aspects—Christianity. 2. Ambition. I. Title.
BV4598.3.H38   2010
248.4—dc22   2009047369

Crossway is a publishing ministry of Good News Publishers.

DP		20	19	18	17	16	15	14	13	12	11
15	14	13	12	11	10	9	8	7	6	5	4	3

To my sons,
2nd Lt. Tyler . . . and his li'l bro Asa—
that your ambitions
would prize God's glory above all!

Contents

Foreword

Humble ambition. Is such a thing even possible?

If you'd asked me twenty years ago, I would have said, "I don't think so."

My friend Dave Harvey is one of the men who have helped me see otherwise. Humility doesn't have to quench ambition. And ambition—the right kind—doesn't have to trample humility. In fact, we honor the Savior by cultivating both.

If that surprises you, then you need to meet Dave.

I vividly remember a conversation Dave and I had years ago. We were sitting outside during an afternoon break in a conference we were attending in Coventry, England. For once it wasn't raining, but that's not why my memory of it is so vivid.

Dave and I had no agenda for our time together. We were just good friends talking and laughing, following the conversation wherever it went. But the relaxed scene was quickly infused with passionate vision when we began to talk about the future. We talked about starting new churches and about whether it was appropriate for us to be ambitious in serving the Savior.

I'm sure Dave brought up the topic of ambition, because it wasn't something I'd given much thought to, if any. For myself, I was immediately suspicious of ambition in my life in whatever form it appeared.

But it was obvious to me that Dave had given much careful thought to the subject. He was wary of the temptation to have selfish ambition, but he also had big dreams. He had a holy drive to advance the gospel through church planting. And as we talked, it was obvious I needed to reconsider my assessment of ambition.

Since that afternoon I've had many conversations with Dave about ambition. And today I can heartily commend this book to you.

Now, Dave hasn't been on a personal campaign to write this book. It was only recently that he wondered about writing on ambition, and all his friends encouraged him to do it. We think he's qualified for a number of reasons. Let me give you just a few.

We think Dave is uniquely qualified to write this book because theology shapes his thinking. He's been studying this for years. Gospel-centered, sound doctrine informs his understanding of this topic.

And he hasn't simply studied it with detached, academic interest. Dave is uniquely qualified to write this book because he has also studied his own heart. He pays very careful attention to his own soul, alert for the slightest presence of selfish ambition. In this book he's going to tell you what he's discovered about his heart. It's not flattering stuff. Dave is a humble man, and he'll help you get to know your own heart.

Maybe you're like I was before my conversion, with no discernible ambition at all. Maybe you keep your dreams manageable and tame because it's just easier that way. Or maybe you're more like Dave—full of boundless energy, always looking for the next challenge. And maybe you've seen your own ambitions turn ugly, as dreams morph into demands and life becomes a quest for personal glory.

Either way, this book is for you. You see, this book is about much more than selfish ambition. This book is about grace. It's about ambition for the glory of Another. It's about seeing ambition rescued and sanctified for the advance of the gospel and the service of your local church, your family, your office, your school. It's about igniting ambition for the glory of God.

Every one of us is ambitious for something or someone. (Yep, that includes you.) But too few of us have thought biblically about ambition. We don't like to talk about it. We assume that if we avoid the topic, we'll avoid temptation. We need someone to talk with, someone to teach us about our aspirations. This book will help you cultivate holy ambition.

So if you think, like I once did, that humility and ambition can't coexist, turn the page. I think years from now you'll remember where you were when you first read this book and what a difference it made in your life.

C. J. Mahaney
Sovereign Grace Ministries

Introduction:
Ambition's Face

Welcome to the introduction—the why-should-I-stop-my-busy-life-to-start-reading-this section. An extensive survey (meaning the one I conducted by walking around my office and asking a few people) has conclusively proven that people rarely read introductions. So thanks for bucking the trend.

Let's tackle the curiosity question delivering you here in the first place: Why should you, with so many demands already hijacking your time, read this book? Let me answer that question in a manner befitting a pastor. Cue the story.

For the past couple decades, I had a condition that kept me from sleeping well. The technical term was apnea. My wife called it "snoring-like-all-git-out."

So I went to see the doctor. "I'll remove your uvula," he said, "then you won't snore. You'll sleep better." Now, I didn't even know I had a uvula, but I freaked when he suggested its removal. There's something about doctors, scalpels, and stitches in the throat area that makes one more content to go without sleep.

For some reason, though, I let them do it. They cut out my uvula. And now I can sleep.

But here's something I didn't expect. When I lost my uvula, I found my dreams. You see, because I never slept well, I never dreamed. I know experts would say I dreamed and just didn't know it—but that doesn't matter because I don't ever remember dreaming. Not once. I was dreamless. Even an expert will tell you that's a boring way to spend a night.

I didn't even know I'd lost my dreams until I found them—or, rather, they were returned to me. Actually, they were rescued, airlifted from some cold, lifeless crevice where dreams hibernate until the arrival of deep sleep. Or something like that.

All this may sound strange, but it's true. My dreams were rescued by a guy with a scalpel. Go figure.

Lots of people live that way—you know, without dreams. They move from one day to the next without the refreshing effect of a memorable dream. I can relate. My lack of dreaming was never bad enough to disrupt my life, just enough to turn my nights into slow motion and make my days hazy, like a mist fogging my mental windshield.

But there are dreams we can lose that are much more significant than those I was losing. Not the REM kind of dreams, but the dreams that drive us when we're awake. The dreams that cause us to reach beyond ourselves, to see beyond the present and to live for something more.

If you're having trouble holding on to those types of dreams, that's a real problem. And this book is for you.

The Most Secret Passion?

My friend Andy is a gifted man who grew up with little drive to develop or use his gifts. Be all you can be? Nah. Ambition for Andy was like algebra—he needed enough of it to pass, but any more than that wasn't worth the trouble. Andy preferred a good nap to a new challenge. He didn't have many dreams—or he'd lost the ones he had.

In college, Andy was converted to Christ. His life was no longer his own. He realized that his fruitfulness as a Christian was linked to his dreams and desires for God. Over time Andy's eyes were opened to dreams he'd never had—aspirations for the glory of God. That changed Andy as a man, a husband, a father, a Christian. He saw the connection between dreams—the right kind—and enjoyment, fruitfulness, and glorifying God. That's quite a connection.

What comes to your mind when you think of ambition? Do you see it as something occupying the interest of God?

Those are the kind of dreams I'm talking about in this book. They stir one of the most potent motivations of the human heart: *ambition*. It's the instinctual motivation to aspire to things, to make something happen, to have an impact, to count for something in life.

Herman Melville called ambition "the most secret of all passions."[1] What do you call it? What comes to your mind when you think of ambition? Does the word conjure images of megalomaniacal petty dictators or chew-up-anybody-in-my-way corporate climbers? Or do you see ambition as an important part of great human achievement—the drive behind scientific discovery, political change, artistic excellence?

More importantly, do you see it as something occupying the interest of God?

Do you know what comes to mind when I think of ambition?

Me.

I've always had more of it than I knew what to do with. If it involved a ball, I wanted to be on a winning team. If it involved a group, I wanted to lead. If it involved school, I wanted to leave to go play something with a ball. (Yeah, my ambitions were strong, but they ran pretty shallow.) From early on, I remember wanting to make an impact, to differentiate myself in some way. Gimme the ball, gimme the lead, gimme the wheel—it didn't matter. I just wanted to be somebody creating momentum. And if, in some strange and totally unexpected way, my actions brought attention to *me* . . . then bring it on, baby!

John Adams once spoke of the natural "passion for distinction" we all have—how every person is "strongly actuated by a desire to be seen, heard, talked of, approved and respected."[2] I'm not saying this is a good thing, but it sure was a Dave thing.

Being "first wherever I may be" was an unconscious mantra I repeated with religious fervor. And it's that very struggle with ambition gone bad that led me to write this book.

Maybe you're like me. You have a vision of success that guides your dreams and decisions each day.

Or maybe you're saying, "Nope, I'm with Andy. I'm pretty good at just chillin' with whatever comes along." But ambition, by definition, is about the future, which means it's about all of us. And as we step into the future, whatever it is we're pursuing—whether it's Mr. Right, the corner office, well-behaved kids, successful ministry, or just a long nap—it matters to God.

So does the *reason* we pursue it.

Rescue Operation

The ambition dreams I'm talking about can't be unlocked with a surgical procedure. They need to be rescued. To rescue means to save something, to prevent it from being discarded or harmed. Capsized ships need it; damsels in distress need it; sometimes our economy needs it. Ambition needs it as well.

You see, I believe that ambition—godly ambition, that is—is a noble force for the glory of God. But let's face it: ambition has mostly hovered outside respectability. For church leaders from Augustine to Jonathan Edwards, ambition was synonymous with the love of earthly honor, vainglory, fame-hunting—pretty slimy stuff.

Today's cultural climate doesn't help. The prevailing worldview in the West involves a distrust in big ideas and man's ability to achieve them and the firm belief that objective truth doesn't exist. But when we deny truth, we suffocate ambition. Without truth as a foundation and ideas worth exploring, meandering replaces meaning, confusion trumps conviction, ambivalence swallows aspiration—nothing really matters all that much.

Humility, rightly understood, shouldn't be a
fabric softener on our aspirations.
True humility doesn't kill our dreams;
it provides a guardrail for them.

Ambition must also be rescued from a wrong understanding of humility. That may sound crazy, but I'm serious. I think this issue quenches a lot of evangelical fire. Humility, rightly understood, shouldn't be a fabric softener on our aspirations. When we become too humble to act, we've ceased being biblically humble. True humility doesn't kill our dreams; it provides a guardrail for them, ensuring that they remain on God's road and move in the direction of his glory.

Ultimately, it's we ourselves who hold ambition hostage. We're sinners, we love ourselves, we aspire to bring glory to ourselves, and we'll drop godly dreams if something more attractive shows up—and in the process, the right kind of dreams die.

So this book is my own little attempt at a rescue operation. The idea is to save ambition—specifically, godly ambition—and return it to where it belongs. To do this, we must snatch ambition from the dust heap of failed motivations and put it to work for the glory of God.

What About You?

Whether you view yourself as a Dave or an Andy, ambitious or laid-back, proactive or reactive, type A or type C, whether you're a student, housewife, executive, politician, or pastor, whether you're staring at a life of opportunities or of limitations, how you relate to ambition will define what you do and who you become far more than you might realize. "One way to clarify your spirituality," says Donald Whitney, "is to clarify your ambition."[3]

I'm not rooting this perspective in common sense or well-researched psychological studies. Nope, ambition is inherent in who we are before the God who created us. The Bible teaches that people are created by God to desire—and to go after those desires with single-minded determination. It's this capacity to desire and strive that can generate remarkable good or stupefying evil. Whether it's to conquer nations or control the remote, we're hardwired to be ambitious for what we want.

Why read this book? Read it to make connections between what you want and what you do . . . between your present opportunities and your future hopes . . . between your life and God's glory. These connections rescue us from fruitlessness, pointlessness, purposelessness, and the haunting gray twilight of wasted time and lost opportunity. They remind us that a big God uses small people to steer the course of history—people like you and me.

To understand ambition, we must understand that each of us lives on a quest for glory. Where we find it determines the success of our quest.

And that's where our journey begins.

1
Ambition Conceived
WE ARE WIRED FOR GLORY

Along the River Wye in Wales, there's a little market town known as Hay-on-Wye. This quaint village has earned an international reputation for its rather unusual trade—buying and selling used books. With more than thirty used bookstores within a square mile (one occupying an entire castle), this place embodies storybook charm.

My friend Pete, an Irish Englishman living in Wales, frequented the town and its bookshops for years. He arrived each time with a single goal: to excavate the theology sections and unearth an original copy of *Lectures to My Students* by the great nineteenth-century preacher Charles Spurgeon. But Pete wouldn't settle for just any original copy; he wanted one signed by Spurgeon's wife, Susannah.

What's with the signature? This remarkable woman was bedridden for much of her marriage but somehow managed to start a ministry called the Book Fund. Seeking to serve her husband and their church in the cause of the gospel, Susannah provided free copies of Spurgeon's books to pastors all over the world. Before they went out, she typically personalized them with her own signature.

Pete figured a few of these copies had endured a century of use and would eventually turn up in Hay-on-Wye. The keys to their discovery, he told me, were patience, perseverance, and a keen eye. This guy was like Indiana Jones on a used book safari.

On a visit with Pete to Hay-on-Wye, I stood in the theology section of a bookshop as my friend recounted his quest to find his treasure. As a first-timer to this Holy Land of Used Books, I was just honored to make the pilgrimage. I was also impressed with Pete's dedication. To search for an original-edition Spurgeon book is a true measure of theological devotion. But to return to Hay-on-Wye time and time again to rescue a book with a symbolic signature makes its own statement. Here was someone willing to pursue a valued prize with uncommon devotion.

There among the shelves, as Pete chronicled his tale of miles traveled and hours logged in his still-fruitless search for Susannah, my vision focused on a book perched on the shelf behind his shoulder. Slipping his gaze for a second, I squinted at the title. Sure enough, staring back at me was a dusty copy of *Lectures to My Students*. I reached over his shoulder and pulled the book from the shelf. Without interrupting Pete's continuing narration, I flipped open the worn cover and glanced down.

You guessed it. In the rookie hands of this Hay-on-Wye greenhorn was an original copy of *Lectures to My Students* signed by Susannah Spurgeon. A smile crept across my face. Oh boy, this was gonna be good.

One of my greatest privileges in ministry is working with churches in the United Kingdom. But these mates describe Americans as a bunch of illiterates who sack the English language like a lordless fiefdom. Since I don't know what a lordless fiefdom is, I usually just smile and nod. But right then I knew one thing: in less than sixty seconds I had nabbed this treasure for which my well-versed Irish-English-Welsh friend had spent years searching.

While Pete kept talking, I held out the opened cover and said with my best Philadelphian Shakespeare, "Yo, dude, is this what you're looking for?"

Score one for the Yanks.

We Chase What We Love

What's stayed with me most about that experience was not the astounded look on Pete's face, nor the smile as it dawned on him that the treasure was finally in his hands, but the quest itself. Pete wasn't just looking for an old book to add to his collection. He wanted to rescue something that had value beyond appearance, value that connected it to something that mattered to him in a deeply personal way.

Pete's story points to something fundamental about each of us. We're pursuers—we go after things we value.

What is it for you? Think about what you value. Maybe you can rattle off your priorities like a shopping list—God, marriage, family, work, peace—these often top the charts. But do they actually define how you live? Or are there some bottom-dweller items on the list that actually get headliner attention?

We're pursuers—we go after things we value.
What is it for you?

If you're not sure, look at how you spend your time, your money. Consider what you think about, where your mind drifts, what you notice and ponder. When all is said and done, what we actually go after is what truly matters to us.

Motown captured it in "Ain't No Mountain High Enough." If we love it . . . *no wind, no rain, no winter's cold can stop us.* That's just another way to say we all chase what we love. It's something in the way we're wired. Be it books, Broadway, or Botox, we pursue what we value. And what does all of this have to do with Brits in bookstores or pursuing what we value? Good question. Keep reading.

Recognizing this impulse isn't a big deal. The trick is getting a handle on how deep it runs and how much it determines what we do. This impulse is so big, it can determine how we respond to Jesus himself.

A Story of Glory

John 12 gives us a window into how this human hardwiring works— this impulse to pursue what we value. After Jesus arrives for the final time in Jerusalem, the scene that quickly unfolds is pivotal in the drama of redemption. He's the center of attention—everybody's attention.

In the middle of it all, Jesus prays, "Father, glorify your name." Immediately a response booms out. "Then a voice came from heaven: 'I have glorified it, and I will glorify it again'" (v. 28).

A voice from heaven! When was the last time you heard someone's prayers get answered at once with the audible voice of God?

One would expect this episode would permanently turn all the bystanders into Christ's followers, right?

Not exactly.

John goes on to tell us something shocking: "Though he had done so many signs before them, *they still did not believe in him*" (v. 37). Surprised to hear that people could be with him—and hear God speak to him—and still not believe? It gets worse. There were others who did believe, yet still wouldn't follow. "Many even of the authorities believed in him, but for fear of the Pharisees they did not confess it" (v. 42).

Let's track this: they listened to him, they believed in him—but they wouldn't say so publicly.

How come? What was so important that they could look straight at the Son of God and turn away?

John says it was "for fear of the Pharisees." After all, these so-called believers were "authorities" in the Jewish community, which meant their jobs and reputations were tied to synagogue life—and the Pharisees could put them out of the synagogue. To be bounced from the synagogue meant you could kiss your position and your income good-bye. That's pretty serious.

Before we judge them too severely, though, think about whether your own conversion carried any fear of reprisals. My decision to follow Jesus was a response to an altar call—several, actually. The possibility of being expelled from my neighborhood was inconceivable, although there were certainly incidents at school where expulsion seemed possible. If the fear those Jerusalem authorities felt was anything like mine during those episodes, I'm sure they were freaked out.

But here's the grabber. In the very next sentence God restrains our instinctive sympathy for these guys by flipping the light on their true motives. Why the hypocrisy? Was it something they *feared*? Yes, at first glance.

But deep inside it was really something they *loved*.

"They loved the glory that comes from man," John writes, "more than the glory that comes from God" (v. 43).

Glory. They craved it. They were addicted to it. Their drive was so powerful, it diverted them from the Son of God himself.

We're Glory Chasers

John is offering us amazing insight into the way we tick: we love glory. We were created to look for it and to love it when we find it.

A lot of glory is being promised and delivered in this section of Scripture. The idea of glory occurs at least seven times in John 12.[1] Glory also remains a significant theme for the remainder of John's Gospel. John wants us to understand that everyone in this scene, including Jesus himself, is pursuing something—and that something is glory.

What is glory? The New Testament word—*doxa*—speaks of worth and dignity and weight. It's most often applied to God but also includes man.[2] Glory is about radiance and splendor. But glory isn't just an attribute; it exists to be seen and recognized. It's about reputation, esteem, standing, honor. At its core, glory is about inherent value that's recognizable to others. It draws attention. Like a magnet, the value of glory attracts us.

The Bible presents us with a God who is glorious in himself (Ex. 33:18–22; Isa. 42:8; 48:11; 60:1–2; Rev. 21:23) and whose glory is recognized and acknowledged (Ex. 15:6; Ps. 66:2; 76:4; 145:5). In a profound sense, this glorious God created the cosmos to display his glory, his worth, his value.

To whom? To a special creature who could take it in, make some sense of it, and rejoice over the worth of his Creator—to us! That's what the Bible means when it calls us to glorify God. We can't make him something he already is—glorious. But we can recognize the glory that radiates from him, value it properly, and give God his due.

That's why we were created. The Westminster Divines understood this. "Man's chief end," they said, is tied to our glory instinct; it's "to glorify God and enjoy him forever."[3]

You've probably heard of storm chasers. They're people who dedicate their lives to running after storms, even at great risk to themselves. If a tornado is barreling down on some Midwestern town, these lunatics are speeding up the road to catch it. They're in pursuit of this spectacular force of nature.

Maybe you don't chase tornadoes, but we're all born glory chasers. Glory moments stir us. Think about what prompts your elation.

Your favorite team wins the championship. You read about a blind man climbing Mount Everest. You watch an Olympic gymnast dismounting flawlessly to grab the gold. You learn that Beethoven would sit down and improvise pieces at the piano that witnesses swear were finer than his written compositions.[4] You hear the story again of Wilberforce prevailing over Parliament to end the slave trade.

We're awed by great comebacks, heroic efforts, sacrificial endurance, and extraordinary gifts. Glory arrests our attention.

My friend Paul Tripp describes us as "glory junkies":

> Admit it. You're a glory junkie. That's why you like the 360-degree, between-the-legs slam dunk, or that amazing hand-beaded formal gown, or the seven-layer triple-chocolate mousse cake. It's why you're attracted to the hugeness of a mountain range or the multi-hued splendor of the sunset. You were hardwired by your Creator for a glory orientation. It is inescapable. It's in your genes.[5]

Glory grabs us. But even more than that, it arouses something in our souls. It stirs us. We experience something totally vicarious, some strange exercise in identification. And make no mistake, it goes deep. It calls to something we value. To do something that matters. To seek something greater than our own puny existence.

It's an instinct for glory.

It pops up in a stark contrast Paul portrays in Romans between two groups of seekers. On one side are "those who by patience in well-doing *seek for glory* and honor and immortality"; on the other side, "those who are *self-seeking*." To the first group, God "will give eternal life"; for the second, "there will be wrath and fury" (Rom. 2:6–8).

God doesn't oppose glory-seeking;
he *commends* it. And what's more astounding,
he rewards it with eternal life.

Try to wrap your brain around this: God doesn't oppose glory-seeking; he *commends* it. And what's more astounding, he rewards it with eternal life.

But there's a condition. We must seek a certain *type* of glory. We're to hunger, crave, earnestly desire—to be ambitious for—the glory that comes from God.

So where do we discover it?

Growing up, my next-door neighbor had a swimming pool. This was before the idea of "a pool in every backyard" was invented. This pool was awesome in how it attracted children. I mean, kids bused in all the way from Idaho just to have a swim. Pools had that effect back then. They gathered kids into one place.

If we want the glory that comes from God, we must begin at the place where it gathered.

This Glory Is a Person

I was converted in college, sometime around 1979. I've met people who know the day and hour of their conversion, their spiritual birthday. That's cool. But it didn't happen that way for me. God's grace was ultimately irresistible, but I can be pretty stubborn, so I resisted to the point of exhaustion. I think fatigue played a prominent role in my conversion. It's probably why I don't remember when I became a Christian.

But there are memories I treasure from that time, all of them centering on a surprising joy in becoming captivated with the person of Jesus. Reading the Gospels was a life-transforming experience—seeing his holiness, his love, his miracles, his kindness. It was entrancing. Jesus wasn't theoretical or abstract, like the logic class I was finding totally illogical. He was amazing, real, alive, and accessible.

Before, I used to think, *If God would just appear to me in glory, I could finally believe.* He did appear—Jesus Christ is the glory that comes from God.

Loving this glory that comes from God means first savoring the One who personified God's glory, Jesus Christ. Glory isn't simply a quality of Christ: Jane has a nice smile, Ronnie's tall, and oh, by the way, Jesus has glory. No, Jesus *embodies* the glory of God. He literally *is* the glory that comes from God.

This is why, in opening his Gospel, John leaves no doubt that glory is on his mind: "The Word became flesh and dwelt among us, and *we have seen his glory*, glory as of the only Son from the Father, full of grace and truth" (1:14). John later notes that even Isaiah saw the glory of Jesus and testified of him (12:41).

Paul and James both call Jesus "the Lord of glory" (1 Cor. 2:8; James 2:1). Paul speaks eloquently of "the glory of God in the face of Jesus Christ" (2 Cor. 4:6), and the writer of Hebrews says of him, "He *is* the radiance of the glory of God" (1:3).

God's glory—his honor, his esteem, his mind-blowing perfection, his incomprehensible value—is embodied in flesh and blood, in the person of Jesus Christ. This is where God's glory gathers.

To love the glory that comes from God means we love the person of Jesus Christ. To love Christ means we value him more than anything else. This is the defining characteristic of Christian conversion—we love the Savior and want to live for his glory. We want to follow him, obey him, trust him, and proclaim him.

But loving the glory that comes from God isn't just an emotional attraction for Jesus. These days spirituality is trending positive, and Jesus is considered pretty hip. But you can have good feelings about Jesus and be far from his glory. To love God's glory means connecting Jesus, the person of God's glory, to Calvary, the summit of God's glory.

Remember when Jesus prayed in John 12, "Father, glorify your name"? Heaven's response was twofold. "I have glorified it," God said, testifying to the fact that his glory is incarnate in the Son. But the Father didn't stop there. He continued, "I will glorify it again."

When would the Father glorify his own name *again*? He was speaking of the atoning death Jesus was anticipating at that very moment.

God was most glorified when the Lord of glory
was crucified on the cross.

We know this because Jesus immediately explained it to his listeners. He said, "And I, when I am lifted up from the earth, will draw all people to myself." John follows up to make sure we get it: "He said this," John explains, "to show by what kind of death he was going to die" (12:32–33). God's magnificence, the magnetic power of his glory, was on full display at the summit of Calvary. God was most glorified when the Lord of glory was crucified on the cross.[6]

As John Stott writes,

> The gospel is Christ crucified, His finished work on the cross. And to preach the gospel is publicly to portray Christ as crucified. The gospel is not good news primarily of a baby in a manger, a young man at a carpenter's bench, a preacher in the fields of Galilee, or even an empty tomb. The gospel concerns Christ upon His cross. Only when Christ is "openly displayed upon his cross" is the gospel preached.[7]

Contemplating the cross, we're left to stand and wonder at this chilling spectacle. The Lord of glory hung upon a cross of shame. Bearing the wrath we deserved, God displayed his love "so that he might be just and the justifier of the one who has faith in Jesus" (Rom. 3:26). On the wings of this remarkable, incomprehensible historical event, God's glory soared ad infinitum.

The cross is amazing because it aligns our mind and heart to the right direction. It's there that we discover the pinnacle of God's glory in the person and work of Jesus Christ. To trust this redemptive act of love as sufficient to save us is the defining step toward loving the glory that comes from God.

But there's something else.

As a new Christian, something happened deep inside of me. My motivation was converted. Grace ignited godly ambition. Ambivalence was replaced with aspiration. I went from thinking apathy was cool to itching to show my faith by my works (James 2:20–26). Literally. At one time God wasn't even on my radar; now I wanted God to use my life to make a difference. Why? Because to be "born again" is to be given a fresh start, to be propelled out of an old life into the adventure of new ambition. Jonathan Edwards called it "a holy ardency and vigor in the actings of grace."[8]

Spurgeon pictures it this way, in a sermon on being "A Good Soldier of Christ Jesus" (2 Tim. 2:3):

> The true soldier is an ambitious being. He pants for honor, seeks for glory. On the field of strife he gathers his laurels, and amidst a

thousand dangers he reaps renown. The Christian is fired by higher ambitions than any earthly warrior ever knew. He sees a crown that can never fade. He loves a King who best of all is worthy to be served. He has a motive within him which moves him to the noble deeds—a Divine spirit impelling him to the most self-sacrificing actions.[9]

Grace fires the soul and makes us want to live for the only glory that matters.

But too often, even after our conversion, in spite of the magnificence of this glory that emanates from God and centers on the cross, we love man-made glory instead. We follow the choice the Jewish authorities made: to love glory from man rather than glory from God.

We will always pursue glory. The only question is, *Where will we find it?*

As John paints this scene for us, what he's bringing to light—and what is absolutely crucial to our understanding of ambition—is that we will always pursue glory. The only question is, *Where will we find it?* Will we love the glory that comes from God, or will we love other glories?

Jesus asks all of us, "How can you believe, when you receive glory from one another and do not seek the glory that comes from the only God?" (John 5:44).

The stakes are high. Ambivalence toward Christ actually means we're rejecting the glory that comes from God in pursuit of something counterfeit. The authorities and Pharisees provide a stunning reminder that one can be sincerely religious and still chase bogus glory.

How about you? You may be searching for glory in dozens of places—but have you found the only glory that lasts?

This Glory Demands a Pursuit

How does this hardwired glory instinct create ambition?

It works like this: To love glory is to pursue glory. If we love the glory that comes from God, it translates into a lifelong, passionate, zealous quest—in other words, godly ambition.

God's love is always seen in his action. "For God so loved the world, that he gave his only Son" (John 3:16). God loved us, so he came after us in Christ. It's the same with us. If I say to my wife Kimm, "I love you!" but I don't pursue her, things will get awfully chilly around the Harvey house. The depth of my love is seen in the intensity of my pursuit.

I once saw an advertisement for the Olympic Games that featured a picture of a runner perched on his mark. Sweat crowned his forehead, intensity filling his unblinking eyes, and his muscles were taut, ready to detonate at the sound of the gun. Beneath the picture was this caption: "He's waited his entire life for the next ten seconds."

What motivates Olympic athletes to train for years for one event—in some cases, for just seconds of actual competition? It's the same thing that kept my friend Pete nosing around old bookstores for years. It's the same thing that makes a person venture out of a comfortable job to start a new business. We see it in the artist who spends day after day in a studio chipping away at a block of stone. Look closely and you'll find it in the shopper who passes up the good deal in search of the best deal. It's one of the things that makes us most human. We consciously pursue what we value.

It's not simply a matter of being driven by biology or genetics or environmental conditioning to satisfy instinctive cravings. Rather, we perceive something, prize it at a certain value, then pursue it according to that assigned value because we were created that way. This ability to perceive, prize, and pursue is part of our essential humanness, and it's the essence of ambition.

Before we'll see godly ambition as worth rescuing, we need to rediscover its value. Simply put, if we understand ambition as God intends it, we'll see how valuable it is and why it's worth the storm-chaser-like devotion to rescue it.

So let's explore how ambition works.

AMBITION PERCEIVES

The seeds of ambition are sown when we perceive value. Something seems worthy of our attention. It attracts us. Value is alluring; our curiosity comes alive.

I once visited the Tower of London and saw the crown jewels.

They were . . . well, wow! Magnificent, incredible, (as my kids would have said)—splendiferous.

Naturally, I just had to get a price check. "So what are they worth?" I asked the guard standing there.

With absolutely no eye contact, yet speaking loudly enough for all England to hear, he announced, "Priceless, sir."

I figured he thought I was deaf. In reality, he knew I was dumb. And dumb rarely gets it. Assuming he didn't understand me the first time, I spoke again. "No, I mean what are they WORTH?" Adding volume always helps. "You know, *STREET VALUE?*"

He must live for these moments. Some fresh "dumb tourist" jokes he can trade at the local pub. Still making no eye contact, he announced even louder, "PRICELESS, SIR!"

The second time I got the translation: "You're not worth eye contact, ya dumb Yank! Don't you understand what you're looking at?"

Okay, so call me clueless. I walked away a little embarrassed, but even more impressed. In his irritatingly smarmy way, the guard was helping me perceive the value beyond what I was seeing.

Perceiving true value is the starting point for godly ambition. We'll never be ambitious for what we don't value. We must perceive God's glory as infinitely more precious than the crown jewels. This isn't easy, because we live in a world that throws a lot of things in our face that appear glorious—wealth, reputation, success, things we'll talk about in upcoming chapters. Our hearts love to look for glory in the wrong places. But perceiving true value in God's glory isn't just important—it's "priceless, sir."

AMBITION PRIZES

Perceiving worth is an important start, but it rarely converts into ambition unless we personally prize what we perceive. We not only perceive worth in something, but we set our desires to possess it. Our affections follow our perception.

Few of us wake up each morning ambitious for exercise. It's also not enough to perceive its value. We can, after all, objectively value exercise but live a couch potato life. For exercise to make a difference, we must prize it as good for us. Ambitions rise to what we prize. If you *perceive* exercise as good, you'll admire people who do it. If you *prize* exercise, you'll rise to do it yourself.

A few years ago a university in Philadelphia owned a well-known painting by artist Thomas Eakins called *The Gross Clinic*. It was so named because it depicts a famous nineteenth-century Philadelphia surgeon, a Dr. Gross (I'm serious), performing surgery on a patient's leg. Seeing this graphic painting you might think it's called *The Gross Clinic* for a more obvious reason. Nevertheless, it's considered a masterpiece of American art and a treasure of Philadelphia history.

But the university was strapped for cash and agreed to sell the painting to two museums in another part of the country. After much civic outrage and a remarkable public and private fund-raising campaign, our two most prominent local museums jointly purchased the painting for more than it was worth on the open market. Why? Because *this* painting was deemed to have a value to *this* city that made it worth more to *us* than simply its value on the market. As they say in the art world, it was a "prized" work of art.

Ambition is willing to pay more than full price if that's what it takes. And whether it's God or golf clubs or a painting of Dr. Gross, we always *pursue* what we prize.

AMBITION PURSUES

There are always things we might value, things we can make an effort to obtain. But ambition isn't just being "in the market" for something. Ambition is prizing something so much that we go after it; we're willing to sacrifice to get it. The value I personally assign to it creates motivation and moves me to take action to obtain it.

God is pleased when we prize and pursue the right things. As the ancient church patriarch Clement said, "It will not be pleasing to God himself if we value least those things which are worth most."[10] That's why we're called to "hunger and thirst for righteousness" (Matt. 5:6) and to "seek first the kingdom of God and his righteousness" (Matt. 6:33). Prizing what is of eternal value stirs ambitions to pursue those things.

In Matthew 13, Jesus illustrates the inestimable worth of the kingdom of God with a couple of little parables.

> The kingdom of heaven is like treasure hidden in a field, which a man found and covered up. Then in his joy he goes and sells all that he has and buys that field.
>
> Again, the kingdom of heaven is like a merchant in search of fine pearls, who, on finding one pearl of great value, went and sold all that he had and bought it. (13:44–46)

What's the link between these two? Both describe something of obviously immense worth. And both describe an unabashed, aggressive, go-for-it-with-everything-you've-got pursuit of prized objects. Jesus is teaching that some things are so valuable, they're worth spending and being spent to acquire.

Paul shows us what it is that's so worthy. "I count everything as loss because of the surpassing worth of knowing Christ Jesus my Lord," he tells us. "For his sake I have suffered the loss of all things . . ." (Phil. 3:8). He's referring to all that once defined him—his people, his education, his godliness under the law, his religious zeal. These cultural crowns of ancestry and accomplishments, Paul declares, are only a big zero compared to knowing Christ.

This, in turn, drives Paul to go after what he prizes with all he has: "*I press on* toward the goal for the prize of the upward call of God in Christ Jesus" (3:14).

Pursuing Christ isn't about withdrawing to a cave somewhere so we can contemplate his grandeur. Pursuit means passion, purpose, and action. It's always moving forward, like Paul. He told the Romans, "From Jerusalem and all the way around to Illyricum I have fulfilled the ministry of the gospel of Christ." Knowing his work had ended in those places, he was ambitious to see the gospel advance to new areas: "And thus *I make it my ambition* to preach the gospel, not where Christ has already been named, lest I build on someone else's foundation" (Rom. 15:19–20). Godly ambition is like that—a completed job isn't a completed life. There are new fields, new ideas, new innovations, new songs, new ways to glorify God.

Connections

"Dave, you don't understand," I can hear you saying. "I'm not like Paul or Peter or Joan of Arc or any other go-getter, do-gooder, bigger-than-life characters that fill the pages of history. I don't even like history! I don't need to be always doing or thinking. I enjoy just *being*. Being alive, being happy, being free—that's my default setting. I don't need to rescue ambition; I wouldn't even know what to do with it if it were hand-delivered to my door."

That's okay. I think this book will open you up to ways of life, happiness, and freedom you've never experienced.

Or maybe you're the type A personality who's kept a to-do list since you were ten years old. You were going to win Olympic gold, make a million dollars, then start a software company that would relegate Apple or Google to ancient history. You've always wanted to lead, to create momentum, to leave people talking about you after you're gone.

That's okay too. I think this book will open your eyes to dreams even bigger than the ones you already have.

Or maybe you're somewhere in between.

Wherever you're starting from, right now I want you to make three simple connections.

Your pursuits—whatever they may be—reveal what you prize.

First, consider that your pursuits—whatever they may be—reveal what you prize. No one can color themselves outside the lines of ambition. "Ambition," says John Stott, "concerns our goals in life and our incentives for pursuing them. A person's ambition is what makes him 'tick'; it uncovers the mainspring of his actions, his secret inner motivation."[11]

Second, reading this book says something about you. You're not reading a magazine or a blog or a popular self-help book right now. Think about it: you perceive areas where change is necessary, and you prize growth enough to pursue this topic. God has incited your interest because God wants to speak to you.

Third, consider that what we pursue will ultimately define us. It will claim our time, absorb our resources, and shape our future.

We perceive, we prize, we pursue. We have ambition.

Back to Glory

Recognizing this universal human tendency to perceive, prize, and pursue, a biblical view of life connects ambition with the God-implanted desire for glory. We were created to be ambitious for God's glory and to take action in pursuit of it. God's Word catches us glory-chasers in pursuit of counterfeit splendor and sets us on a chase for the real thing.

As Paul sets forth at the beginning of his magisterial presentation of the gospel in Romans 1, God is at the center of all glory—he's the value of all values. The problem Jesus ultimately came to solve was how to rescue sinners from the grip of a glory exchange. As Paul states it, we "exchanged the glory of the immortal God" for that which was neither immortal nor God (1:23).

It's an either/or dilemma. We pursued the glory of man rather than the glory of God. We valued man above God and launched a high-speed chase in the wrong direction—with eternally disastrous consequences.

The good news of the gospel is
that we aren't trapped by the tragedy of
misplaced glory.

But the good news of the gospel is that we aren't trapped by the tragedy of misplaced glory. While our ambitious impulses led us to vain pursuits, the Lord of glory has come to rescue our ambition. He has come to redeem us and recapture us for his glory. Where we haven't perceived the difference between true and false glory, he opens our eyes to behold the glory of God in the face of Jesus Christ. Where we haven't prized that which has real value, he recalibrates our desires to fit his direction. And where we've pursued false glory, he turns us and sets our feet on the path of righteousness for his name's sake—for his glory.

In his classic devotional *The Life of God in the Soul of Man,*

Henry Scougal pictures a life transformed by an ambition set on God's glory.

> He who, with a generous and holy ambition, hath raised his eyes toward that uncreated beauty and goodness, and fixed his affection there, is quite of another spirit, of a more excellent and heroic temper than the rest of the world.[12]

In this first chapter, perhaps you've made a vital discovery: *you are ambitious!* Perhaps you're also thinking that your ambitions are hardly "of a more excellent and heroic temper than the rest of the world."

I can relate. I would describe my ambitions as imperfect and seriously un-heroic. And that's on a good day. Maybe the kind of ambition Scougal describes seems more like a pipe dream to us.

But that's why we've joined together on this journey. We're in for quite a ride.

Do you think Pete was surprised when I handed him that Spurgeon book with Susannah's signature? That's nothing compared to where we're going next. If you dare, we'll probe what happens when we locate *ourselves* at the center of our dreams and drives.

Yes, we were created for glory, wired for it. That means these haphazard ambitions we all share must have a meaningful purpose. To discover that purpose, we'll explore how they were corrupted, then how they're rescued. Then we'll see how rescued ambition can find expression in ways that might surprise you.

Are you intrigued (or shall we say, "ambitious") enough to continue?

2
Ambition Corrupted
GROWING SMALLER IN OUR ATTEMPT
TO BE GREAT

For a twenty-year-old, he was pretty ambitious. No, scratch that. When your goal is to conquer the world, you've left ambitious for "Burn the incense and torch the sacrifices—*I want to be worshiped!*"

More audacious than his dream was the fact that Alexander the Great almost achieved it. From the Balkans to the Nile to the Himalayas, he forced together a vast empire over three continents and two million square miles. Calling himself "the Great" may have been pretentious, but Alexander had serious game to back it up. The historian Plutarch tells a fascinating story of another young man named Julius Caesar. After reading about Alexander's exploits, Caesar grew quiet and suddenly burst into tears. His friends asked why. "Alexander at my age had conquered so many nations," he cried, "and I have all this time done nothing that is memorable."[1]

For some, life's deepest ache is that of unfulfilled ambition.

We've learned that the instinct for glory is God-given and resides within each of us. So if ambition is good, then Alexander's ambition (and young Caesar's too) was good, right?

Not exactly. Scripture actually speaks of a form of ambition that spoils its goodness by removing God as the goal. The Bible calls it "selfish ambition," and it makes a debut all the way back "in the beginning."

Shrinking Ourselves
The living God launches human history in the role of Creator. He methodically executes his will in a six-day artistic adventure

culminating in the formation of man and woman. For these first people, made in God's image, life is simple and good. God is their Father, and Eden is their home. Adam's mandate is clear: Be fruitful and multiply, and rule, subdue, exercise dominion over creation (which begins with naming all the animals). The world's first job description is a hefty one.

Adam was called to a glorious ambition—to spend his time and talents for God's glory.

But that abruptly changes. Preening in paradise is the Serpent, the earthly form of a fallen one, Satan. He was the original glory thief, and his crime downsized him from angel to devil. Now he's skulking in Eden with one goal: to steal glory belonging to God.

So Satan starts asking questions, making claims. He begins to distort truth about God, to subtly erode confidence in him and to replace it with ravenous, self-seeking desire—to turn Adam and Eve's attention from the many good things God has given to the few things God prohibited. "Why can't you eat from the tree?" he asks. "For God knows that when you eat of it your eyes will be opened, and *you will be like God*, knowing good and evil" (Gen. 3:5).

Notice how Satan baits the hook of distortion and seduction with the tasty morsel of forbidden glory: "You will be like God." Or in the simple logic of serpent-speak, "Guys, why work God's farm when you can have your own spread? You can get the ultimate promotion—be your own boss! Think about it: He doesn't have any glory that can't be yours. But since he's withholding, take things into your own hands. *Eat the fruit!*"

Eve bit hard, then handed it to her hungry husband. The world would never be the same.

At that moment the glorious ambition to use God's gifts for God's glory shriveled beyond recognition. Replacing it was self-confined glory. Adam and Eve were now on a quest for glory apart from God, driven by a hunger for self-exaltation.

That's what the Bible calls sin—the universal human drive to disregard God's moral law and live independent of him. Sin happens when we outwardly transgress the law, but it also happens when we disobey in our hearts, even if we obey with our actions. Sin is rebellion that leads to alienation. Sin is cosmic treason and a deadly cancer in the soul. Sin blinds us, and it drives us. Left unchecked, sin will destroy us, and we'll be judged eternally for it.

Sin does the same thing to us that it did to Adam and Eve. It distorts the truth of God and undermines our essential dependence on him. It seduces us to crave things that deface God's holiness and assault his glory. Ultimately, sin moves self to the center of our desires and dreams. Rather than promoting God's order and glory, we become relentless self-promoters. It's a condition that shrinks the soul.

Listen to how Jonathan Edwards diagnoses it:

> The ruin that the Fall brought upon the soul of man consists very much in his losing the nobler and more benevolent principles of his nature, and falling wholly under the power and government of self-love. Before, and as God created him, he was exalted and noble, and generous; but now he is debased, and ignoble, and selfish. Immediately upon the fall, the mind of man shrank from its primitive greatness and expandedness, to an exceeding smallness and contractedness.[2]

I know those words are dense. But they're worth understanding. Track this: Adam and Eve's ambition for promotion actually had the opposite effect. Detached from God, their love dwindled and their souls shrank. Their world became no bigger than themselves. Man became his own quest—a life expedition to move self to the center of his motivations.

We grow small trying to be great.

If you're like me and prefer an "Edwards-for-Dummies" version, here's how someone else worded it: "We grow small trying to be great."[3]

Can you relate to that?

I can. Earlier I mentioned my struggle with the wrong kinds of ambition. I call them "Davebitions." So often I'm Davebitious. I assume that my family would work much better if they all majored in Daveology. Friendships work best if they have a Davetistic bent. I believe many of life's misunderstandings could be cleared up with just a few Daveological insights. Overall the world would be a better place if we could just celebrate an annual Davetoberfest.

I guess you can call me a Daveaholic. There, I've said it. I feel so much better.[4]

Now, before you let yourself off the hook and offer prayers for my suffering wife and family, think about this. The reason I'm a Daveaholic is not temperament or because I was deprived of something as a child. I didn't get this from my environment. I got it from my ancestors—Adam and Eve. And since we all share the same ancestors, you got it too. The problem—the reason we're all engaged in a quest for self-confined glory—is sin.[5]

The early church used a fascinating visual to describe the self-preoccupying nature of sin: *incurvatus in se*.[6] It means we "curve in on ourselves." In the service of self, our desires boomerang. When a hard-wired desire for glory is infected with *incurvatus in se*, noble ambitions collapse. The quest for self-glory rules the day—as it did that day in Eden. In our desire to be great, we actually shrink ourselves.

Since this is a common tendency for us all, how do we recognize it, and how do we deal with it?

Building Monuments to Me

Funny thing about fallen ambition: when it curves in, it gathers energy to launch out.

"At the age of six I wanted to be a cook," artist Salvador Dalí once said. "At seven I wanted to be Napoleon. And my ambition has been growing ever since."[7] Ambition has a driving tendency to push outward to amass new glory. But instead of launching great deeds in the service of God, we're more likely to launch massive monument-building campaigns for ourselves.

In his epistle, James brings a sober assessment to this zeal for self-expansion:

> Who is wise and understanding among you? By his good conduct let him show his works in the meekness of wisdom. But if you have bitter jealousy and *selfish ambition* in your hearts, do not boast and be false

to the truth. This is not the wisdom that comes down from above, but is earthly, unspiritual, demonic. For where jealousy and *selfish ambition* exist, there will be disorder and every vile practice. (3:13–16)

James gives my glory-swiping a name: "selfish ambition." This is ambition gone wrong. And he says it's a symptom of the wrong kind of wisdom—the kind the Serpent offered Eve in the garden.

In this part of his letter, James is teaching people how to live with each other in reasonable harmony. So he drops a pop quiz on the class: *Who is wise among you?* The answer is, you'll know the wise by their works. Conduct reveals wisdom. Suddenly it's a take-home test. James wants folks to look at their lives. What will they see? There are only two possible answers.

They may see "wisdom from above," which is "pure, then peaceable, gentle, open to reason," and a bunch of other wonderful things that make for harmonious relationships (3:17–18).

Or they'll see that other kind of "wisdom"—the kind that's "earthly" and "unspiritual" (3:15). This wisdom from below goes beyond nasty to "demonic." It's a word that points to the author of ambition-gone-bad, Satan himself. When self-glory is the axis of our ambitions, we repeat the first-ever coup attempt when Lucifer tried to depose God and steal his glory. And the results are always grim.

The biblical word for selfish ambition portrays those who, like prostitutes or corrupt politicians, demean themselves for gain.

Interestingly, the original word here for "selfish ambition"—*eritheia*—portrays those who, like prostitutes or corrupt politicians, demean themselves for gain. It underscores the idea that our self-exalting behavior falls back upon us, shrinking our soul.

John Chrysostom, one of the great preachers of the early church, once said, "Men who are in love with applause have their spirits starved not only when they are blamed offhand, but even when they fail to be constantly praised."[8]

Have you ever met people who are starving their souls in their search for praise? You know who I'm talking about—the person who holds court with his ideas or always manages to center himself into conversations. Convinced that others are captivated, his vocabulary takes flight as he discovers new ways to describe old wars.

Have you ever noticed how often our stories are just that—*our* stories? We become the cast, the script, and the plot, and our name's in all the credits. We're on a quest for constant praise. And in the process we starve our souls.

I've had some soul-starving moments. Recently one of the men from the team of pastors I serve with was telling me about a new initiative the team wanted to undertake. I thought it was a great idea. In fact I thought it was a great idea a couple of months ago when *I* thought of it and suggested it in the first place! Now *my idea* was being relayed back to me as if it had arrived by courier from some distant planet. Or maybe it just seemed that way. But there was no reference to me, my ideas, my greatness and glory. Nothing. Injustices like this must be answered.

Maybe you're thinking, "What did you do, Mr. Author-of-this-chapter-on-selfish-ambition? Did you quietly whisper thanks to God that, wherever the idea originated, there seemed to be common vision on an important initiative? Did you recognize that credit isn't important anyway, that what's important is that the church is being served? Did you remember that even if you did suggest it first, you probably got the idea from someone else?"

Not for a second. *My idea* demanded that I speak. But because my friend is discerning and would have flagged any overt grab for glory, I chose the more subtle, nuanced approach. Carefully referencing my prior conversations and convictions, I dubbed the idea wise, then added my appreciation for how the men around me are so easy to lead. *Real smooth, Dave.* That's what you call savvy politics.

No, that's what you call raw, selfish ambition.

God was faithful to convict me for my inordinate desire to receive credit for my idea. When I look back, I see myself sitting in my chair across from my friend. Like a hot air balloon, I'm there trying to inflate myself quickly so I can rise in the eyes of my friend. The sheer stupidity wallops me all over again as I write these sentences. There was a lot of effort in that conversation to make myself big. But smaller was all I got. Mercifully, my friend was generous to forgive when I confessed to him a few days later.

As James points out, the fact that we starve our souls in the search for praise doesn't mean that our selfish ambition is confined. James paints the ugly picture in verse 16: "For where jealousy and selfish ambition exist, there will be disorder and every vile practice." Selfish ambition doesn't travel alone. It has a partner in crime: jealousy. And the two of them inevitably pick up a couple more gangsters: disorder and vile practices. The Greek words for these last two terms speak of instability or confusion and morally worthless deeds. These qualities are like a gang, always traveling together, looking for trouble. Where selfish ambition hangs out, jealousy and disorder and moral worthlessness are cracking their knuckles, ready to rumble.

In other words, selfish ambition guarantees negative consequences.

Good Ambition Gone Bad

Selfish ambition doesn't always start that way. Sometimes ambition starts out well. All sorts of valuable things might stir our desire, and we begin to move toward them. In the passage we looked at above, James isn't addressing folks hoping for disorder. He is writing to people who had chosen to follow Christ at the potential loss of everything. In response to the gospel, and in the face of growing disapproval, they committed themselves to the church community. Some kind of godly ambition was churning within them.

But now something has started to stink. You see, ambition sours easily. Like milk, it may look fine from the outside, but you can smell it going bad. Disorder is a consequence of aspirations gone sour— selfish ambition.

How does it happen?

Back in the spring of 1814, Timothy Dwight (a grandson of Jonathan Edwards and the president of Yale College) gave the baccalaureate address to Yale's graduating class of future leaders. This wasn't the typical "your life is limited only by your dreams" graduation address. Dwight chose this key moment in the lives of these graduates to sound a warning "On the Love of Distinction."

He wisely pointed out this snare on the path of success, an ingredient that could curdle the sweet milk of their achievement. "Wickedness," he said, "can in no other form become more intense, nor its plans more vast, nor its obstinacy more enduring, nor its destruction more extensive, or more dreadful" than the love of distinction.[9]

> The love of distinction has a certain appeal for everyone, whatever our vocation.

Dwight's warning is relevant to us all. The love of distinction has a certain appeal for everyone, whether our vocation is full-time parenting or the pastorate, whether we're gunning for tenure or for high school quarterback. It promises that you'll stand out in the minds of people and in the market of skill and ability. It declares that joy and fulfillment await the man or woman who can achieve the highest goal: distinction for self.

However, like every good lie containing a morsel of truth, the love of distinction doesn't have the payoff it promises. Dwight continued:

> But among all the passions which mislead, endanger, and harass the mind, none is more hostile to its peace, none more blind, none more delirious than the love of distinction.[10]

The love of distinction never has a project, purpose, or person in mind beyond self. The most important thing isn't the success of a business or a great endeavor. The most important thing is that *I* be remembered for being the best, for being first. It's the trap on the path of ambition.

> Selfishness is in its nature little and base. But no passion and no pursuits are more absolutely selfish than the love of distinction. One's self is here the sole object; and in this object all the labors, pursuits, and wishes terminate.[11]

We've all seen the ruin brought about by the love of self-distinction. Enter Wanda Holloway, the Texas woman who sought to hire a hit man to knock off the mother of her daughter's cheerleading rival. Enter Tonya Harding, who plotted the injury of her leading rival for a figure skating championship. Enter the salesperson neglecting family to land that account, or the politician selling his office to get that next party nod. Enter the athlete juicing up to hit farther, run faster. All are filled with ambition for distinction.

> How terrible must be the account given of life spent only in laboring to acquire distinction. Adam indulged this disposition once and lost his immortality. Satan indulged this disposition once and was cast out of heaven. What will become of him who has eagerly followed this career of his apostate first parent and of this apostate angel throughout the whole of his probation?[12]

Love of distinction sometimes looks innocent. But it's what brought death to Adam, and it's what got Satan kicked out of heaven. This is pretty serious stuff.

Forget Alexander—I'm Dave the Great

Whether it's blatant or subtle, selfish ambition always leads me to the same place: I become a glory thief, swiping attention from God and demanding greatness for myself.

Sometimes it gets pretty bad. I want to claim King Solomon's boast: "I became great and surpassed all who were before me" (Eccles. 2:9). Yeah, who wants to be just "good" or "equal"? "Great" and "surpassing all" sounds so much better. Come on, folks, crown me the Sultan of Awesome and parade me through the streets filled with people yelling my name. Make sure everyone's there from my old neighborhood who ever dared question my greatness. I'll capture it on Facebook for anyone who missed it.

Pretty sad, huh?

I wholeheartedly agree with Timothy Dwight. Any man or woman who indulges this self-centered passion is in a hopeless state. I can testify personally that nothing is more absurd than acting as if we, like Alexander, have our own "the Great" at the end of our names. Just look at some of the titles of greatness I've found in my own campaigns of personal glory.

Dave the Occasionally Great. This Dave has his moments. He even surprises himself sometimes. He'll do something selfless, think about others before himself. He'll have sympathy for people in need. He'll be moved by images of poverty and oppression on the news, and even give to worthy causes. The problem is, he just can't string it together—the self-focused, self-absorbed Dave keeps showing up as well. This Dave can confuse others, and he certainly confuses himself. Greatness is hit or miss. And the misses can be biggies.

Dave the Great-in-His-Own-Mind. This Dave thinks great thoughts—about Dave. He has wonderful plans—for Dave. He can always think of a way to do it better than the other guy. He's ready to offer his valuable opinion about anything. Just ask. Sometimes you don't even need to ask; his opinions just topple out like golden nuggets from an overstuffed treasure chest.

Dave the Potentially Great. This is the guy everybody says could really do something if he put his mind to it. He has the tools; he just needs to put it all together. But this Dave fears success and the responsibility that comes with it. Better to always "have potential" than to risk anything—just keep pushing success out there into the future, and nobody can criticize you for how you achieved it.

Dave the Formerly Great. This Dave has been there and done that. He'll talk about the way things were "back in the day." He thinks everything's gone downhill ever since . . . well, ever since things were great. Dave the Formerly Great can have a selective memory: his failures fade away, while his accomplishments are easily recalled—and easily exaggerated.

Dave the Comparatively Great. This Dave is always a seven out of ten. Not perfect, but certainly better than average. Dave the Comparatively Great is extremely conscious of the competition. He knows what it takes to stay ahead of the average guy. This Dave doesn't appreciate somebody being promoted over him. It messes up his comparison index. He loves to win, hates to lose.

Dave the Tomorrow-I'll-Be-Great. This Dave has great intentions. He's just about to do something; he can feel it. He just has to get a little more rested up first, a little more organized, a little more motivated. Ask this Dave why he still hasn't done what he said he'd do, and he turns into . . .

Dave the If-Only Great. This Dave really wants to be great, but he just can't catch a break. He's constantly being thwarted in his great endeavors by the decisions, weaknesses, or failures of others. If only he could find people to count on . . . if only people were more predictable . . . if only he had the resources or the time or the help, he'd be truly great. If only.

Dave the I'd-Be-Great-If-Others-Would-Just-Notice. This Dave would never claim to be great, but would sure appreciate it if others would perceive his effort. He knows what people like, and he's good at delivering it. If he had to choose between some great success that only God noticed and some small success witnessed by others, he'd choose the latter every day and twice on Sunday. It's not that he doesn't care whether God notices; it just feels better when other people do.

Dave the I'll-Be-Great-If-It-Kills-Me. This Dave is so motivated for greatness that he's fixated on his goals. He pushes hard and won't take no for an answer. Failure's just not an option.

The Darkness beyond Greatness

What do all these Daves have in common? Instability. Confusion. Disorder. Morally worthless deeds. Jealousy. *Selfish ambition.* Greatness lost, smallness attained.

Have you met any of these Daves? Maybe you see a Dave-like resemblance in your own life.

Ambition is a tricky thing, isn't it? We think greatness is attainable, so we work hard to attain it. But, like Alexander, as soon as we think we've reached it, we discover something greater beyond our reach. There's always a nicer lawn in the neighborhood, a smarter kid in the class, a better golfer on the course, a more esteemed brother or sister in the church.

So we're tempted to despair—the despair of the not-as-great-as-we-want-to-be. Charles Spurgeon's epitaph on Alexander could easily describe one way we can go:

> See Alexander's tears! He weeps! Yes, he weeps for another world to conquer! Ambition is insatiable! The gain of the whole world is not enough. Surely to become a universal monarch, is to make one's self universally miserable.[13]

Sound depressing?

There's another option. We can simply lower the standard of greatness to fit what we can reliably attain.

Live a holy life? *Impossible.* How about a balanced and reasonably moral one? *Done!*

Love God and others wholeheartedly? *Forget it.* How about a head-nod to God and tolerance toward others? *Done!*

Obey God's Word as the rule of my life? *Too restrictive.* How about leafing through it to find words that make me feel better about myself? *Done!*

Our failure to achieve greatness is far more dangerous than we think.

But whether our ambition sends us into despair or leads us to settle for near-great, there's something with which we must contend: Our failure to achieve greatness is far greater, and far more dangerous, than we think.

You see, the standard of greatness isn't set by us. It's set by God. And God doesn't grade on a curve. He doesn't reward a good try. Why? Because he demands perfection. That's the true definition of greatness, of true glory. It's perfection.

Alexander could have conquered the whole world and gone on to build a city on the moon. But great as he was, he could never be perfect.

Deeply embedded in my sinful flesh is a desire to install myself as lord over all. I want my name worshiped, my glory exalted, and my fame talked about long after I'm dead. But by pursuing this selfish ambition, we fall short, tragically short of the greatness and glory of God. As the apostle Paul puts it (far too absolutely for my preferences), "*for all have sinned and fall short of the glory of God*" (Rom. 3:23).

And in the way God judges things, in our falling short of God's greatness, we fall under his wrath. Apart from perfection, there's no other possibility.

The bad news we've been driving to in this chapter is this: my quest for my own greatness leads me to a dangerous place. In our hyped-up pursuit of self-glory we place ourselves in the path of the wrath of God.

So we're in desperate need of rescue. We need to be freed from this wrath against imperfection—and we need to be rescued from ourselves. We need to be rescued from our own chronic imperfection.

We need to obtain perfection from somewhere outside ourselves. That's what the next chapter's all about.

3

Ambition Converted

WHERE TO GO WHEN YOUR BEST AIN'T
GOOD ENOUGH

"Golf," says Alistair Cooke, "is an open exhibition of overweening ambition, courage deflated by stupidity, skill scoured by a whiff of arrogance."

Let me tell you about a time I had a perfect round of golf. Perfect for my world, that is.

Now, let me be clear—I'm not a golfer. Typically a perfect round of golf is the one I play in my mind. When I do play, breaking one hundred strokes on eighteen holes requires a very liberal approach to math. Or cheating. Or a substitute player. Breaking one hundred on nine holes is slightly more manageable. Slightly. Which takes us back to my perfect round.

Someone once said that golf can best be defined as an endless series of tragedies obscured by the occasional miracle. My miracle happened on a nine-hole "executive" course—which sounds like a place for real important people but actually means that it's a smaller course with lower expectations.

My first drive went straight as an arrow, with just as much fairway on the left as on the right. That's remarkable, because my first drives are usually humbling; they're often a lot like a divining rod, able to find water where none appears to be. But on this day my approach had a touch of backspin and put me on the green, putting for birdie. Though I missed my first putt, I tapped in for par and immediately considered quitting for the day. It wasn't going to get better than that.

But it did. On each hole I was increasingly amazed by what my clubs were doing and where the ball was going.

For me, a good day of golf is scoring 60 for nine holes. If you're a non-golfer, that means you're better than me. A great day is when I shoot par on a single hole. But at the end of this day's Miracle on the Links, my score totaled a 38—close to par for *the whole round*.

In my world, that's perfection.

What's your definition of perfection? A completed to-do list? A weedless lawn? A balanced budget? Abs of steel?

As we've seen, ambition is a drive toward glory, a drive toward greatness. Ambition implies a standard, a "par" for whatever course of life we're on. If we achieve it, we can rightly view ourselves as successful. If we don't, we feel like failures.

The bad news of the last chapter is that there's an eternal standard to which we're held—a standard not for "par" but for perfection. And perfection is a standard that's beyond our ability to attain. For our ambition to be anything more than a frustrating and futile experience of wasted effort in the face of impending judgment, we must not rely on our own efforts toward perfection. We need to be given perfection by someone else.

The gospel announces that this is exactly what has happened. If you're a Christian, you're never more loved or accepted by God than at this exact moment. What a remarkable truth! But this acceptance didn't come cheap. It was purchased for us when God substituted his Son for us upon the cross—what we call the atonement. In a divine swap, Christ took our sin and gave us his righteousness. Martin Luther called it "the wonderful exchange."[1] This remarkable display of love takes us to the heart of the Christian gospel.

When we talk about the gospel, we center our attention on the atoning death of Christ for our sins. Yet the gospel is even more than this. It includes the life of Christ as well. And though this may sound odd, Christ's perfectly lived life is essential to our understanding God's approval and why ambition now matters to God.

Perfection for Us

We looked earlier at the sweeping statement in Romans 3 that we've all fallen short of God's glory. The entire book of Romans is a theological tour de force celebrating the what and why of our salvation. Drawing from the Old Testament, Paul helps us see the broader story line of God's intention to slay his Son to save sinners.

In the first four chapters of Romans, Paul lays out why we've fallen short of God's glory and why we're unable to solve the problem ourselves. Chapter 5 gives us a fascinating angle on this rescue mission—a contrast between Adam, our selfishly ambitious forefather, and Jesus Christ. "For as by the one man's disobedience the many were made sinners," Paul writes, "so by the one man's obedience the many will be made righteous" (v. 19).

By one man's obedience . . . many will be made righteous. What does Paul mean? He's making a comparison, setting up Christ's perfect obedience against Adam's disobedience.

Paul wants us to know that Christ's obedience was not some irrelevant footnote in Scripture. It was important. Real important. There's no question in Paul's mind: Christ's obedience mattered. It was huge. But we need to understand why.

When we think about Christ's obedience, we often think first of his death. Certainly Christ's obedience includes the cross. In fact, John Piper calls it "the crowning act of his obedience."[2] His willingness to pray, "Not my will, but yours, be done" (Luke 22:42) and then to carry that conviction through the agony of crucifixion—it's incomprehensible.

Christ's obedience included a life in which he obeyed God's law in all things, at all times.

But Christ's obedience also included a life in which he obeyed all of God's law, in all things, at all times.[3] He didn't just have a few surprisingly perfect days, like mine at the golf course. Every day was perfect for Jesus. It was a lifetime of hole-in-ones. Our Savior lived in perfect alignment to the will and law of God.

Think about that for a second. From his birth in a stable onward, it was thirty-three years of perfect obedience. Now that's a mind-bender.

Guys much smarter than me have labeled this "the active obedience of Christ."[4] Earlier we talked about his substitutionary death, but the active obedience of Christ introduces another astonishing idea: his substitutionary *life*. Jerry Bridges has said:

> For the most part Jesus' life of perfect obedience has been seen only as a necessary precondition to His death. The truth is, however, *Jesus not only died for us, He also lived for us.* That is, all that Christ did in both His life and death, He did in our place as our substitute.[5]

I got my seminary education at Westminster Theological Seminary in Philadelphia. Westminster was founded in 1929 by J. Gresham Machen after Princeton Seminary had given way to the liberal theology of the day. Years later, when Dr. Machen lay dying, it's said that he dictated a telegram to his longtime friend John Murray, professor of systematic theology at the seminary. Short and simple, it said, "I'm so thankful for the active obedience of Christ. No hope without it."[6]

Why would a dying theologian, with a powerful mind that could open numerous doctrinal windows in that moment, look specifically to the obedience of Christ as a source of hope? Because the obedience of Christ matters . . . a lot. Let's look at why.

Understanding the Transfer

Think back to when you responded in faith to the gospel. Did you experience a weight of guilt removed after your conversion? Many people do.

But were you aware that there was also something given to you, something you desperately needed and still need every day?

Imagine an elderly retiree of modest means getting a letter from the Internal Revenue Service reporting that he has underpaid his taxes every year since the age of eighteen. Thanks to interest and penalties, the unpaid taxes add up to an exorbitant debt he can never repay. Unless some miracle takes place, he's going to jail!

The man arrives on his court date fully expecting to be found guilty and sentenced for what he owes. Suddenly there's commotion around the judge's bench. Something shocking is happening. The judge quiets the court to make an announcement. Someone who loves the man has paid his debt. The judge declares him not guilty.

In his amazement, the man's knees buckle.

But there's something else, the judge says. The man's benefactor also transferred ten trillion dollars into his bank account.

It's incomprehensible, but the man has gone from guilty to wealthy. In the blink of an eye, the problems of guilt and his standing before the court were permanently reversed. Not only was his guilt removed, but it was actually replaced by an overflowing bank account. He entered the courtroom guilty; he left rich beyond his wildest imagination.

We were in far deeper trouble than the guy who got hauled into court. In Adam's disobedience we all fell. "One trespass led to condemnation for all men," Paul expressed it; "by the one man's disobedience the many were made sinners" (Rom. 5:18–19). So we have a double problem: we inherited Adam's guilt, and on top of that we have enough guilt and debt of our own to condemn us.

To fix this problem, we certainly needed a Savior who could take away the problem of what we owe. And that's exactly what Jesus has done. Do you believe it? *Jesus paid it all, all to him I owe*.[7]

In college, my oldest son was in an ROTC program. The military training was rigorous for him, but it provided nice benefits for me. We paid nothing for his tuition, room, books, pencils—it was a full ride. Each semester I got a statement from the school that itemized all the expenses. At the bottom the costs were tallied, and in the "You Owe" box it always said "$0." I loved that zero.

But when a sinner stands before a holy God, it's not enough to have a zero in the "sin" box.

An absence of sin is not a ticket for an audience with God.

The clearing of our debt was a job half done. We needed something more than the removal of guilt. We also needed a Savior who could give us the perfection we did not possess.

The righteousness necessary for God's approval had to meet specific criteria. Nothing less would suffice than a life of perfect obedience, fully satisfying all the demands of the law. We've all had days like my Miracle on the Links, but we've never done *every* shot right—a hole in one every time. We've never obeyed God *completely*, not even for a day.

A holy and righteous God, by definition, cannot allow anything presented before him that isn't holy and righteous. An absence of sin is impressive when compared to the gunk in my heart, but it's not a ticket for an audience with God. We needed to be "made righteous" (Rom. 5:19). We need a record of perfect obedience to God's law. It's absolutely required. Only a declaration of righteousness would permanently secure God's approval and pleasure.

Enter the Perfect Man, Jesus Christ.[8]

In Adam's failure, we all failed. But Christ came to do what Adam did not. As "the second Adam," Christ met the demands of the law. He sustained perfect obedience over an entire life, and even through death. For God's plan to work, Christ had to succeed where Adam failed. He did. And we won.

His record of obedience in life and death formed the account of righteousness transferred to us at the cross. The death of Christ removed our debt and returned us to a zero balance. And the obedience of Christ put unimaginable wealth into our bank account. "By the one man's obedience many [were] made righteous." A positive righteousness—a transfer of the riches of Christ's righteousness to us—was needed to open a way for a holy God to accept us. We needed righteousness, tons of it. And we got it.

Think about this. Works matter. We needed to be saved by works—not ours but Jesus Christ's! R. C. Sproul says:

> The only way anyone can ever be saved is by works. God requires that His law be fulfilled. And unless you possess perfect righteousness, you will never be justified. Now the issue is this: By whose works will you be justified? Justification by faith alone means that we're justified by the works of Christ alone.[9]

On his deathbed, Machen understood his condition with stark clarity. Stripped of everything but his fading flesh, he knew who he was apart from Christ. He was a son of Adam, an inheritor of what Adam left behind for him. That means he was a product of the fall of Adam into disobedience and sin. In himself he was due at any moment to stand before the judgment seat of God—naked, guilty, and hopeless. But Jesus Christ clothed him with the righteousness he needed for his upcoming appointment. Every step Jesus took away from temptation, every turned cheek he offered, every angry thought he averted—all the wealth of those righteous responses was placed in Machen's account. He wasn't just "not guilty," but declared righteous, all because of "one man's obedience."

So what does that mean for me and my ambitions?

The Perfect Man Rescues the Motive of Ambition

Let me ask a question: if we're Christians, what does God see when he looks at us?

Is it our flaws and failures? Driving over the speed limit? Shading the truth? That outburst of anger or lust? What comes first on God's score sheet?

It's true, we stand before God as men and women filled with ambition for our own glory—so much so that we try to rob God of his. And yet we stand as recipients of Christ's record of perfect obedience. God didn't ignore our sin. He judged it by pouring out his wrath on his Son. Christ took our punishment and gave us his righteousness.

So what does God see? He looks past our sin to Christ's sinlessness. He literally sees thirty-three years of Christ's perfect works dripping off of us. Since Christ lived a perfect life and died a perfect death so that his perfect record of righteousness could be credited to imperfect sinners, this perfect record is what God sees when he looks at us.

No wonder Paul says,

> *Blessed* are those whose lawless deeds are forgiven, and whose sins are covered; *blessed* is the man against whom the Lord will not count his sin. (Rom. 4:7–8)

Understanding this magnificent truth will transform how you think about your dreams.

Apart from God, our quest for greatness is often a search for approval. I want to be applauded and esteemed. I live for praise. I attempt great things because I crave being celebrated. Selfish ambition is often a desperate quest for an earthly "Atta-boy," a drive to fashion a world that worships me.

Our search for approval is over. In Christ, we already have all the approval we need.

The gospel brings me explosive news: my search for approval is over. In Christ I already have all the approval I need.

Because Christ's righteousness has been transferred to me, all the time and energy I once squandered trying to be liked or praised or to achieve something to validate my existence can now be redirected toward doing things for God's glory. I no longer live *for* approval; I live *from* approval.

Let me reiterate this good news, in case it hasn't sunk in. The riches of Christ's obedience in life and death are what God sees when he looks at us. He no longer sees us wallowing in our naked grabs for glory, in our lies, lusts, or fears. Christ's record of perfect obedience now frames God's vision of our existence.

And God is never ambivalent in the face of perfect righteousness and holiness. He celebrates it. Like the father watching his son hammer a home run or a mom discovering her daughter's perfect report card, God's acceptance is spontaneous, instantaneous, enthusiastic, and permanent. His pleasure and approval surges toward us, carrying all the spiritual blessings deserved by Christ.

I was at a soccer game once when a kid scored a goal. His father was so enraptured by the event that he began screaming his approval and celebrating his son's triumph. But this guy wouldn't stop. I was waiting for him to run out and carry the kid off the field on his shoulders. That's heady stuff for a kid who can barely tie his shoes. And I think their team lost.

But losing didn't matter. What the old man saw in his son sparked spontaneous, enthusiastic, and loud approval for his son.

Does this mean God doesn't care about a believer's sin? Absolutely not. That would be unbiblical, as well as wrongheaded. As Christians, sin doesn't touch our standing before God, but it can definitely affect our experience of God. When I lied to my dad as a kid, he didn't stop being my father. But it sure did affect our relationship. My experience of his affection changed. His love was expressed in another way, a more painful way. The hand that often blessed me converted to a hand of discipline.[10] I felt his displeasure, though I never stopped being his son.

Make no mistake. Sin is real, and we can sin away a lot of good stuff. Sin robs our joy in God. It's a delight-smasher. But sin never alters or reverses what Christ did upon the cross. It never causes God to withdraw his name or his acceptance from us.

So the rescue of godly ambition is now under way.

Do you struggle with the paralysis of analysis, unable to act boldly because you're wondering what people will think? Do you fear falling short of your goals or that God will somehow be displeased with you for not doing what he really wanted you to do?

You stand in the righteousness of Christ—and you possess all the approval you'll ever need. Don't spend another moment trying to be great in the eyes of men. Instead, *be ambitious.*

The Perfect Man Rescues the Obedience of Ambition

Christ's perfect obedience not only rescues us from the vain search for approval but also makes our obedience possible. Because God accepts us in Christ, we can now act in imitation of Christ.

In the opening words of the Sermon on the Mount (Matthew 5), Jesus holds out blessings for those who walk as he walked. The New Testament Epistles not only celebrate the gospel but also call us to apply it. We're being renewed in the image of God to represent Christ on this earth. We walk in the reality of what has been imputed to us.

This means it's important for us to consider what obedience meant for Christ.

Jesus was God—eternal, co-Creator, "the image of the invisible God, the firstborn of all creation" (Col. 1:15). Creation answers to him, angels announced his arrival, every knee will bow to him (Phil.

2:9–10). And yet, when he came to his own people, they didn't receive him (John 1:10–11). God became man in Christ. He strolled the earth essentially unrecognized, no one ever fully getting it. In the end, he was deserted by even the closest of his friends, the very ones for whom he was dying.

Now consider these words from Isaiah: "He was despised and rejected by men . . . as one from whom men hide their faces he was despised, and we esteemed him not" (53:3). The living God becomes man, and *that's* how we treat him.

I remember walking through an airport when a famous sports star was passing through. A horde of people orbited; he was the main attraction—instantly recognizable by the crowd. Everybody wanted in on the action. When God became man in Christ, he deserved a blockbuster media campaign that would splash his name all over the world. What he got was a crucifixion.

Has there ever been a time when you didn't get the glory you thought you deserved?

Has there ever been a time when you didn't get the glory you thought you deserved? Maybe your ministry in the church wasn't acknowledged, or a coworker "borrowed" your idea, or the kids failed to appreciate your daily service in their lives. Did you feel a sense of injustice, anger, the desire to set things right by wrenching heads in the direction of your sacrifice?

Let's face it: some of our worst moments are how we respond when people don't give us what we think we deserve. But we're called to obey God by imitating the one who, when despised, returned kindness. When rejected, he showed love. When misunderstood, he remained patient.

Every day of his life, he pleased God with every thought and every action. I'm never close to being able to say that, even on my best days.

But here's the kicker: Christ said we're to respond to life the same way he did.

He understands our struggles. Christ "in every respect has been tempted as we are, yet without sin" (Heb. 4:15). We're intentionally snubbed? Christ knows what it's like. People ignore our contribution? Christ understands. We have to deal with someone who must have been absent when God dispensed the courtesy and respect gene? Christ experienced the same temptations that boil up within us. Rejection, people who disappoint, forgotten efforts—he was tempted in every way we are, "yet without sin."

Christ also empowers us to do what he calls us to do. We'll be rejected, misunderstood, mistreated simply because of our association with him. Being ambitious for the glory of God isn't an easy thing. We'll face opposition from the fallen world around us and, certainly, from the remaining sin in our hearts. But Christ has come to live in and through us by the Holy Spirit. We pursue the glory of One who understands our weaknesses and has made provision for them.

Do you want to walk in the power of God? *Be ambitious.*

The Perfect Man Rescues the Joy of Ambition

At the cross our status changed. With it came the one thing we most need to pursue a life of godly ambitions: the approval of God. It's no wonder William Carey said we should expect great things from God and attempt great things for God.[11] He understood that approval should inspire ambition.

And here's the marvelous mercy that Christ's obedience secures: it clears the way for us to experience true joy in ambition.

Formerly our aspirations were the soul-shrinking agents of self-exaltation. But because of Jesus, everything has changed. Having God's approval changes why we obey, aspire, and apply. Now aspiration fuels delight. We can pursue great things for God, and it will enhance our joy in God.

We no longer live ambitious for approval, but we act ambitious because we have approval. Here's the difference: One disillusions us, the other inspires us. One is temporary, the other permanent. One drives us, the other delights us.

From time to time you'll hear reports about people who strike it rich. Occasionally they keep their jobs, though they no longer need the income. Even then their unexpected wealth has to alter *why* they work. When we're only scraping by, we work for shelter, heat, and a good cheesesteak. But if we're a multimillionaire, we work for pleasure. With all financial needs resolved, work isn't something we have to do, but something we get to do.

It's the same with our ambitions. As the great theologian B. B. Warfield said, "The one antithesis of all the ages is that between the rival formulae: Do this and live, and Live and do this; Do and be saved, and be saved and do."[12] In Christ we live—therefore we do, and do gladly.

As if that weren't enough, our dreams and desires to serve God are rewarded for eternity. How amazing is that? We're rewarded for the accomplishments he enables in the dreams and desires he gives. This is cause for some serious rejoicing.

Do you want to enjoy your life? *Be ambitious.*

The Perfect Man Makes It All Real

I have a friend who goes by the initials C. B., I have another who goes by C. J., and in this chapter I've quoted guys named R. C. and B. B. Not sure what's up with the initial thing, but I like it, since it's easier to spell their names.

My friend C. B. loves to laugh, he loves Philadelphia sports, and most of all he loves Jesus. When C. B. gets excited for Jesus, his face lights up and he rubs his hands together real fast. Sometimes it sounds like sandpaper . . . C. B. sandpaper. If he's real excited, it sounds like C. B. locomotive. You don't want to be in front of a C. B. locomotive because the dude's six feet two and he's got some girth.

People can't enter C. B.'s orbit without being captivated by his love for Jesus. His eyes fill with tears daily as he ponders what Christ has done for him. I envy him for that. My eyes fill up with tears only when I think of being run over by a C. B. locomotive.

C. B.'s a guy who wants to give it all for Jesus, each and every day. Recently I asked him whether he was always like that—passionate for God and zealous to bear fruit. He surprised me by saying he made a profession of faith as a kid but lived his teen years with little spiritual fruit. He had no ambitions for God. He was passionately ambitious about being cool, being tough, being a great athlete, being celebrated by his peers.

One day a youth leader got hold of him. (Thank God for good leaders!) This guy courageously confronted C. B. and told him his ambition for glory was a good thing, but he was looking in the wrong place. The leader said he was chasing false glory and squandering his life.

That's quite a charge, but it hit C. B. square between the eyes.

That night he couldn't sleep. The words haunted him—*squandering your life*. But he didn't just sell his stuff and fly to Asia to work for God. He studied the cross, and he pondered what he learned. He realized that the youth leader was actually kind in his assessment. C. B.'s goal was his own glory. Standing before the cross, he saw himself as a foolish sinner swinging the hammer that nailed Christ to the tree. That busted C. B. up. In fact, it still breaks him today.

The C. B. I know bears no resemblance to that other C. B., except for the passionate ambition. C. B. wants to do some damage for Jesus.

But he says his goal isn't to simply make his life count. His entire orientation to Christianity was rescued by that encounter with the Perfect Man crucified for him. When the cross moved to the center, the goal of his ambitions came into focus. Knowing he had all the approval he needed freed C. B. to attempt great things for God. It wasn't "This is what I must do for God"; it was "Look what Christ has done for me! Now I'll joyfully be spent for him."

Of Golf and Glory

Much as I'd like to, I'll probably never shoot close to par in my life again. More importantly, there are many other things I want to do and should do that will never get done. And there are things I'll do that I may regret. But I don't struggle with fear or guilt over that, and I certainly know better than to try to atone for my failure—on the golf course or anywhere else.

My confidence is in the completed round of another—the Perfect Man, Jesus Christ, my Savior. Like J. Gresham Machen, I know my hope is in his perfect obedience, both for this life of spotty performance and the next life of eternal glory.

As Machen's theological predecessor at Princeton, Charles Hodge, said so well:

It is good to know—especially when facing the next world—that for every time we have failed to conform to God's will in thought, word, and deed, by actively sinning or failing to conform to his revealed will, his Son has fulfilled the obedience that we owe. By never once giving in to the lust, pride, sloth, greed, selfishness, and malice that are so often allowed space in our overcrowded hearts, Jesus Christ becomes our Savior not only in his atoning death but throughout his life.[13]

Christ's finished work on the cross—the fact that he has fulfilled the obedience we owe—changes the purpose of our ambition and obedience. As good stewards, we're now zealous for good works because it coincides with why we were redeemed. "For we are his workmanship, created in Christ Jesus for good works, which God prepared beforehand, that we should walk in them" (Eph. 2:10).

Walking in good works begins with aspiring to good works, being ambitious for them. Dreaming and doing things for God is the evidence, the effect, and the expectation of genuine faith.

We already have all the approval we need. As we begin to explore the glories of godly ambition, let us never leave this solid footing: God's approval comes from the perfect obedience of the Perfect Man.

4
Ambition's Agenda

EVERY AMBITION HAS AN AGENDA—
WHAT'S YOURS?

It has been called the greatest rescue mission of World War II.

During the second half of that war, American bombers were sent on dangerous missions over southern Europe to cripple the oil production feeding the Nazi war machine. Hundreds of crews in flying tin cans would soar over heavily fortified regions into blinding storms of anti-aircraft shells. Navigating through the brutal gauntlet of ground fire, many were forced to bail from their flak-riddled aircraft. Injured airmen often drifted by parachute into occupied Yugoslavia, fully expecting to be captured or killed.

But on the ground below them a remarkable rescue team was already being mobilized. Serbian peasants tracked the path of the floating flight crews. Their sole mission was to corral the flyboys and steal them to safety—all before the Nazis arrived.

Risking their own lives, the peasants fed and sheltered the downed crewmen and cared for their wounds. These rescued men were in friendly hands—but still on enemy soil. They still needed to be rescued.

The story of what became Operation Halyard builds toward a daring mission, a secret landing strip, and a clandestine evacuation plan involving C-47 cargo planes. Amazingly, more than five hundred airmen were rescued—every single man who had been confiscated by a peasant.

Drama, suspense, daring. This has Hollywood blockbuster written all over it. But there's a fascinating subplot to the rescue. To travel to the evacuation site, the airmen were entrusted to Serbian freedom fighters, who alone knew the way to the evacuation site. Despite a language barrier that prevented clear communication, the airmen spent weeks following their guides through unfamiliar terrain—waking and walking on command. The direction, the pace, and the destination were in the hands of their rescuers. The men had been saved from their enemy, but the journey wasn't over. They still had to walk to freedom.

In the last chapter we looked at the ultimate rescue. We used to be glory thieves, swiping honor from God and hoarding it for ourselves. But now, through Christ's death and his life of perfect obedience, we're justified—accepted, approved, and permanently secure in God's love. We no longer need to look for approval; we have all the approval we need. That's some serious good news!

That raises an interesting question. If God sees Christ's wonderful works when he looks at me, isn't that all that matters? Why should I do anything else? Why should I be ambitious for *anything* if the *ultimate thing* has already been given to me?

Saved to Walk

The story of Operation Halyard sheds light on an important spiritual reality. To be rescued *from* something sets us on the path *toward* something.

For the airmen it was a journey of survival. For us it's a journey of faith. The One who saved us is now calling us to walk. It's nonnegotiable. Though snatched from spiritual death, we soon discover that the Christian life isn't an arrival—it's an adventure. We experience a rescue, then we're pointed to a path.

The apostle Paul describes this active view of the Christian life in his letter to the Ephesians, urging them to "walk in a manner worthy of the calling to which you have been called" (4:1). This is a brief command, and it's easy to rush past it. But this isn't a toss-off request. It's the center of Paul's letter, the bridge between truth and life, and it's crucial for us to understand what Paul is saying.

To this point, Paul has spent three chapters of this epistle exulting in what Christ has accomplished for us. The list is stunning:

- We were chosen in Christ (1:4).
- We were predestined for adoption (1:5).

- We've been given an inheritance (1:11).
- We were raised up with Christ (2:6).
- We're reconciled to God (2:16).
- We're blessed with unsearchable riches in Christ (3:8).

And that's just for starters. If you're digging for spiritual treasure, Ephesians 1–3 is a gospel mother lode.

In the final three chapters of Ephesians, Paul looks at the practical implications of what he has said in chapters 1–3—what effect this redemption has on our actions, our words, and our relationships.

In Ephesians 4:1, Paul is building the bridge between doctrine and duty, principle and practice, creed and command. That stunning salvation we've received? We're to live in a way that's appropriate to it. "Walk in a manner worthy of the calling to which you have been called."

Bridges aren't for standing; they're for getting somewhere. And here, on the bridge between the first and second half of Ephesians, we're called to stoke up our ambitions and put on our walking shoes.

Paul is saying, "Synchronize your walk with what Christ has accomplished. Since you're declared righteous, now walk righteous. Since you're declared holy, purify your ambitions and actions." B. B. Warfield describes this as Paul's "ringing appeal . . . to live up to [our] privileges."[1] Become in faith what God has declared you to be in Christ.

Eight Cows and a Worthy Call

Ever heard of Johnny Lingo? He was a character in a short piece of fiction written by Patricia McGerr in 1965. Johnny was Polynesian and one of the sharpest traders in the South Pacific islands. Strong, bright, and rich, he was a leader among the people on the island of Nurabandi.

On the adjacent island of Kiniwata, there lived a woman named Sarita. She was no looker—plain, skinny, and in desperate need of some Mary Kay products. She walked the village with a fretful disposition, shoulders sloping downward as if she carried some unseen burden. But for reasons known only to poets and prophets, Johnny loved Sarita and wanted her as his wife.

It was customary among the people of these islands for a man to buy his wife from her father—sort of a reverse dowry. Two or three cows would secure an average wife. Adding another cow would get you an upgrade; two more would buy a head-turning beauty and some Ginsu knives.

In a transaction shocking the islanders, Johnny shelled out *eight* cows for Sarita. Why pay quadruple the going rate for Sarita? Simple. Johnny wanted her to know that in his eyes she was worth more than any other woman. It was a statement from him of her value. To Johnny, she was an eight-cow wife.

Word of this unprecedented bride price spread far and wide. But that's not the end of the story.

One day a visitor came who had heard the story of Johnny's marriage and wanted to see the bride for herself. When she did, she couldn't believe her eyes. Sarita "was the most beautiful woman I have ever seen," the woman reflected. "The lift of her shoulders, the tilt of her chin, the sparkle of her eyes all spelled a pride to which no one could deny her the right."

Sarita *became* what Johnny declared her to be: an eight-cow wife. She was walking worthy of her call.

> ## We're called to become what God has declared us to be.

Like Sarita, we're called to become what God has declared us to be. Like the stranded airmen in Yugoslavia, we're rescued to start walking. God saved us, adopted us, forgave us, declared us righteous in his sight, and altered our desires so they bend toward him. Then he says to us, "Now become what I have declared you to be."

John Murray puts it well:

> To say to a slave who has not been emancipated, "Do not behave as a slave" is to mock his enslavement. But to say the same to the slave who has been set free is the necessary appeal to put into effect the privileges and rights of his liberation.[2]

Paul begins to explain what walking worthy looks like in the next two verses: ". . . with all humility and gentleness, with patience, bearing with one another in love, eager to maintain the unity of the Spirit in the bond of peace" (Eph. 4:2–3).

We're now called by God to walk consistent with the mind-boggling privileges we enjoy in Christ. Like seasoning in a delicious meal, the knowledge of our redemption permeates our soul and seasons our life with the character of Christ. This is the one thing most worth perceiving, prizing, and pursuing—an ambition essential to our joy, fruitfulness, and endurance in this life.

If God has given us so much, then called us to walk worthy of it, there must be something glorious out there for us. He must have some agenda at work.

God's Agenda for Our Ambition

If you're anything like me, when you think about your calling as a Christian, your thoughts probably go to *What am I going to do for God?* Jake feels called to serve the poor; Maggie's called to nursing; Leroy's called to the mission field; Juanita's called to raise her children, sometimes even her husband. We often view activity and calling as synonymous.

God's glorious agenda for our ambition
begins with *who we are.*

But here's a truth we don't always think about: God's glorious agenda for our ambition, like his glorious gospel, begins not with what we achieve but with *who we are.*

Walking in a manner worthy of the calling to which we've been called means I have a new ambition. Instead of gunning for my own glory or comfort, I'm ambitious for a changed life.

This can be hard to wrap our brains around because we tend to evaluate who we are by what we achieve. That's the trap the rich young ruler fell into when he asked Jesus, "What must I do to be saved?" and got his heart put on display in response. It's the thing

Peter kept stumbling over in his often comical attempts to prove himself to Jesus. It's what I do when I find myself totaling my good deeds done for the day as steps closer to God. But Jesus wasn't impressed with the rich young ruler or with Peter—nor is he all that impressed with me.

The worthy walk commanded in Ephesians 4 is unlike any other trip. This journey works from the inside out. It starts with who we are, then moves to what we do.

That's why Paul begins with qualities like humility, gentleness, patience, and bearing with one another in love (4:2). This is how Christ lived and loved. As his disciples, we follow after him. We walk as he walked. "Whoever says he abides in him ought to walk in the same way in which he walked" (1 John 2:6). This is "the calling to which [we've] been called" (Eph. 4:1).

Make no mistake: ambition for godly change does lead us to *do* things. Future dreams are obtained through ambition for present growth. The goal of Paul's exhortation is to arouse our ambition to apply the gospel to our own lives. Note some other areas Paul brings up in the remainder of Ephesians 4: peace, doctrine, purity, honest labor, holy speech, forgiveness. To experience our best future, we must apply those today. We must take action that accords with the gospel.

In the Pittsburgh neighborhood where I grew up, everyone was a Steelers fan. In fact, if you didn't like the Steelers, you had no business being in Pittsburgh. There were games where the temperature was below zero and the stadium was still sold out. (I didn't say we were bright, just devoted.) But as kids we had few, if any, opportunities to get to the stadium to see the games live. So each Sunday, robed in the sacred black and gold, we would mount our sofas, snacks in hand, and position ourselves to "experience" the game on TV.

Through a mysterious process only armchair athletes can truly understand, we began a symbiotic meld with the players and vicariously participated in the gridiron struggle for yardage. Their first downs became our triumphs, their fumbles our failures. A touchdown prompted high fives and other raw forms of masculine exchange, as if we'd personally pounded the ball across the goal line. We gave 110 percent, but all from the cozy confines of the recliner.

You know, the athlete and the fan share some remarkable similarities:

1. They both breathe.
2. They're both human.
3. They both breathe.

Okay, so fans and players are remarkably different. Fans sit back in the recliner and enjoy the players' performance. Their vantage point is for the most part through the electronic window of the TV, protected from the elements, the chaos, and certainly the pain of the game. With ready access to multiple angles, instant replay, slow motion, stop-action, and real-time play-by-play analysis by trained commentators, fans don't just watch the game—they "experience" it (as HDTV salesmen are eager to tell us). But their perspective is only theoretical. No matter how big the flat-screen TV, fans aren't really playing the game.

Players, by contrast, experience an entirely different day. Being on the field is an immersion in chaos and pain. The players' roles and responsibilities have direct bearing on what happens in each play. A player can't simply hit the fridge or channel surf during timeouts. Unlike the fans, the players' world is one of decision, action, and exertion. Everything they do matters. Their vantage point is a field of activity where they apply what they know.

Football players don't ask fans to join their huddle. Fans live vicariously; players live experientially. Same game, world of difference.

Christians are not fans.

We're called to get off the recliner and to go make a difference in the game.

On the playing field of the real world, we're called to get off the recliner and to go make a difference in the game. When Paul tells us to walk in a manner worthy of our calling, he's grabbing spiritual fans out of their cozy den and putting them on the field of play. He's saying, "Get in the game!"

Thankfully, the gospel gives us all we need to play well; ultimately, not even the outcome is in doubt. But it's not about watching, it's about doing. And the doing of the worthy walk isn't easy. Doing humility is hard—just try responding graciously to a big hit of criticism. Think purity looks good in the playbook? Try running it into the teeth of a blitz of sensual imagery. Committed to the ground game of truth-telling? What if it isn't getting you anywhere? Eager for unity? What will we do when opposition is stacked up against us at the line of scrimmage?

Ambition begins with knowing who we are in Christ and what we're given because of that fact. But it trains itself for the game of life according to the agenda God sets for us. He shapes our ambition for the role he wants us to play in his plan.

God's calling makes me ambitious for a changed heart and a changed life.

How God Shapes our Ambition

God makes our forward momentum his business. That's why so much of Scripture is dedicated to getting us walking, keeping us moving, and ensuring that we finish our course. But if God truly desires our forward momentum, why does it sometimes feel like I'm banging my glass head against a stone wall? My longings for impact are confusing and fragile; I just don't know what I should do. Or maybe I'm not the ambitious type. I hunger for nothing more than a good magazine and a peaceful place to read it.

God has an agenda: it's to change us into the image of his Son. And one way he brings about this change is through our dreams and ambitions. God works in us through that to which we aspire.

Sometimes God brings our dreams to life; sometimes he doesn't. But how we respond to his work becomes an important intersection for change in our lives. As we cooperate with him, we discover that it's not ultimately about nailing the promotion, or raising well-behaved kids, or winning the Daytona 500—as good as all those things may be. It's about something much bigger: how I become like Christ while I pursue those dreams.

Do you understand your relationship with God that way? He doesn't need us to get things done, but he delights to use us, so he must shape us for his service. That's exactly what creates godly ambition—the activity of God in us and around us to ultimately work through us.

Let's look at three important ways he shapes us by dealing with our ambitions.

AMBITION DELAYED

To be alive is to have delayed ambitions. Times when God's to-do list says, "Postpone Dave's dream . . . indefinitely!" Maybe it's graduation, a job, a better job, health, marriage, a promotion, ministry opportunities—a delay in one or more of those areas is an experience common to all.

And it's nothing new. Take a number and stand behind a long list of biblical characters waiting while walking. Abram and Sarai are promised a child of their own but must wait twenty-five years for Isaac's arrival. David is anointed the next king, but he must wait more than a decade while he runs for his life and lives in a cave. Paul is called to evangelize the Gentiles, but not before he punches the clock for fourteen years in the wilderness. It's God's way of doing things. Delaying the fulfillment of our dreams seems to be part of refining and rescuing ambition.

How we live when ambitions are delayed
significantly shapes who we become.

How we live when ambitions are delayed significantly shapes who we become. God uses the wait to teach us to walk in a manner worthy of our calling.

Wait isn't a popular word. We like it about as much as a toddler does. But waiting is a tool God often uses. Scripture is full of waiting—we're taught to wait for God to act (Ps. 25:3; 27:14; 37:7; 130:5; Isa. 49:23; Hos. 12:6), to wait for our adoptions as sons (Rom. 8:23), to wait for the return of the Lord and his righteousness (1 Cor. 1:7; Gal. 5:5; Titus 2:13). We're to wait in faith, knowing that Isaiah's words are true: "From of old no one has heard or perceived by the ear, no eye has seen a God besides you, who acts for those who wait for him" (Isa. 64:4).

Waiting is God's backhoe in the excavation of our ambitions. Waiting unearths and brings to the surface what we really want.

Yet waiting is a strange thing. God's purposes are not a bus stop where we just sit, waiting for the right option to come by. No, we keep walking while we wait, and we wait while we walk. This may sound ironic, but it serves many purposes.

Waiting purifies our ambitions. We may be tempted to think that if our ambitions are delayed, they will fade. This isn't true of authentic godly ambition.

Reach your hand into a river and grab a handful of rocks. You can tell the ones that have been recently deposited and those that have been there for a long time, waiting. The new arrivals are rough with edges and sharp points. The other rocks are smooth; time and water have worn away their rough exterior, revealing a polished, beautiful stone.

For us, waiting has the same effect. God purifies our ambitions by delaying their fulfillment. An ambition with a waiting sign is an ambition being smoothed in a riverbed of God's activity. The rough edges—the selfishness in our ambitions—become smooth. The ambition is purified. The dull exterior starts to shine.

Waiting cultivates patience. If you're like me, you believe patience is a virtue; you just don't want to wait for it. All right, I'm impatient. Impatience tries to act spiritual when it says, "Lord, I want your will for my life, and I want it *now!* Later won't do." Impatience deletes God's schedule and replaces it with our own. It perverts ambition into demands. But God has a rescue plan for us. It's called waiting.

Two centuries ago the young English pastor Charles Simeon aspired to shepherd God's people. He was eventually appointed to the pulpit at Trinity Church in Cambridge. He was delighted, but the people were disgusted. Most of the members opposed his evangelical convictions and were intent on frustrating his ministry. For twelve years their opposition was expressed in a most unusual manner. They actually boycotted the Sunday service and locked the pews so no one else could sit in them. Folks coming to church had to sit in the aisles. During all that time, Simeon preached, pastored, and waited.

How does someone endure that kind of irrational opposition for twelve years?

> In this state of things I saw no remedy but faith and patience. . . . It was painful indeed to see the church, with the exception of the aisles, almost forsaken; but I thought that if God would only give a double blessing to the congregation that did attend, there would on the whole be as much good done as if the congregation were doubled and the blessing limited to only half the amount. This comforted me many, many times, when without such a reflection, I should have sunk under my burden.[3]

Faith and patience prevailed. Charles Simeon eventually saw his pews emancipated and his pastorate at that church blessed for forty-four more years. As Simeon recounted the precious passages that sustained him during those earlier twelve years, he often quoted Lamentations 3:25, "The LORD is good to those who wait for him."

Perhaps in reading this you're becoming aware of impatience toward God and his timing in your life. But is God's timing not perfect? Are his ways not perfect? Is his will not perfect? Is his character not perfect? And hasn't all this perfection been displayed for us in the cross? Who are we to question God in impatience when he has so perfectly displayed his love for us in the shedding of his Son's blood on the cross?

Waiting redefines our definition of productivity. We live in a world where time is money, so speed is essential. We define our success by how "productive" we are, and productivity is wrapped up in activity. We develop daily lists that would take months to accomplish and strive to achieve what no man or woman ever could. We lay our heads on our pillows at night, discouraged about our failure and driven to try harder tomorrow.

Waiting is often God's reorientation program
aimed at our definition of success.

God defines productivity differently. For God, productivity is wrapped up in transformation, in who we're *becoming*, not in what we're accomplishing.

Waiting is often God's reorientation program aimed at our definition of success. He lovingly empties our misguided preoccupation with accomplishment and fills it with ambitions to know him and be like him. God isn't beyond slowing our walk to remind us that only he is omnipotent, and we're not; only he is omnicompetent, and we're not; only he exists without need for rest, and we don't.

Airports are modern conveniences that God uses to help me learn patience. Here's the drill. When entering an airport, we enter a world where flight schedules are contingent upon hundreds, even thousands, of variables outside the airlines' control. An engine malfunction shuts down one flight or one gate, which subsequently stalls the schedules of thousands of people. And there's nothing you or I can do about it. We can whine, rant, or throw a tantrum about needing to be there right now! But the only way to influence when a plane lands is with a heart attack or a bomb threat—neither of which will solve your particular "now" problem. Add to this your early airport arrival to make the flight and the wait for connecting flights, and you quickly realize that learning patience is your only link to sanity.

Waiting takes our definition of productivity to school. It tutors us to connect our agenda not to personal achievement but to God's glory. Then we can bear God's fruit, satisfied that his list is accomplished during our day, even when ours is not. "By this my Father is glorified, that you bear much fruit and so prove to be my disciples" (John 15:8).

Let me encourage you: if people describe you as a workaholic, if people seem like an interruption to goals, if you've been temporarily sidelined by illness or downsizing, or if you have difficulty resting, then cultivate the ambition to study "waiting" and "rest" in Scripture. It will help you "bear much fruit."

AMBITION DEVELOPED

God loves good ambition. It brings him glory as he works through our desires to fulfill his purpose. God doesn't need us, but amazingly he uses us. But to position us for fruitfulness, he's continually working in our lives, turning our desires toward his ends and developing our ambitions in accordance with his will. In the process we become what God has declared us to be in Christ.

Much of the rest of this book will deal with how we cooperate with God's ambition development project in our lives. But let me give you a picture of what it can look like through the experience of my friend David Sacks.

A good ambition becomes a selfish ambition when it's our only ambition. It's called idolatry.

David is a member of our church. He's an artist who enjoys dabbling in many genres but finds his niche in photography. David didn't know that a good ambition becomes a selfish ambition when it's our only ambition. In the Bible that's called idolatry.

Sometimes God must first save us from our ambitions in order to redeem them. To develop our ambition, God first converts it. That was true for David, who describes it this way:

Before conversion, photography functionally controlled me. I moved to New York City to pursue photography and really devoted myself to that; I spent almost every waking moment investing in my photography career. But my life seemed so aimless. My ambitions and goals were wrapped up in achieving success in photography at any cost. I was working many hours every week to make that happen. But as I look back, I remember that season as incredibly hopeless. My identity and sense of worth was all wrapped up in being a successful photographer . . . it was like photography was a god to me. I was obsessed with myself. My only ambition was to make a lot of money and work with a lot of creative, powerful people.

God rescued David and began the work of revolutionizing his value system. Through prayer, the study and preaching of God's Word, and involvement in a local church, David began to change the way he looked at his aspirations. He saw his ambition for art as the idolatrous pursuit that it had become. His drive to succeed didn't disappear. Instead, how he defined success changed. God rewired him for a different kind of glory. David never dreamed there could be so much satisfaction from actually having your greatest ambition undermined.

"I once heard someone say," David recalls, "that when you become a Christian you probably won't be as good at something as you could be, because you're going to spend less time doing it. From one perspective, there's truth to that—and it's for our good. I have a wife and three kids—I want to live according to God's will for my life. And I learned that wrapping my ambitions around God's goals was the only way to achieve success as a husband, father, artist, and Christian."

David discovered the joy of using his gifts not simply as a vocation but also to serve God's people. In addition to his private studio, David now uses his craft to raise money for orphans in Africa while occasionally providing shoots for different ministry causes he supports. Cultivating that ambition has only deepened his delight in the use of his gifts.

"Part of recognizing that the gift is from God is finding ways to use it for God," David says.

> There's joy in that. That's why I love to offer my gift freely at times. Part of the human condition is a continual desire for meaning in life and work. Some of the work I do commercially is lucrative, but doesn't have a lot of inherent meaning in it; it's not enriching people's lives. Doing cover work for Christian publications, or going to Africa or Afghanistan or Ukraine to do photo shoots for ministries, is very much about honoring God's teaching about being a good servant and being a good manager of the talents. That's when we find real meaning.

Do you see what happened to David's ambition? God didn't judge him in his idolatry; he rescued him from it. What amazing love! And God didn't take David's career ambition away; he converted it and developed it. Along the way God used his aspirations to change him. David's dreams developed along lines that gave him joy without causing him to sacrifice those things that really mattered in his life.

God's ambition development projects always produce results for our good and his glory.

AMBITION DENIED

The *Harvard Business Review* called it "middlescence." It's the growing phenomenon among middle-aged workers to be "burned out, bottlenecked and bored."[4] But it's more than that. It's men and women realizing they'll never achieve certain dreams. The manager beginning to realize he'll never be an executive, the technician who feels her sacrifices for work were fruitless, the artist confronting the limitations of gifting, the worker bored stiff while confronting the probability that "this is all there is." "Like adolescence," the *Harvard Business Review* sums it up, "middlescence can be a time of frustration, confusion and alienation."[5]

For David Sacks, walking worthy of his calling as a Christian coincided with success in his other ambitions as well. But sometimes God's agenda for change involves losing our dreams.

For many it goes beyond vocation. The fifty-something single woman concludes she'll probably never marry. The man approaching retirement realizes he doesn't have enough money to retire. Our spouse doesn't change; the marriage is stalled and aimless. We're drifting like a car with no brakes or steering wheel. The kids seem stuck and require too much work. The house or neighborhood or church or social network or—you fill in the blank—no longer satisfies. "We don't realize how influential our dreams are until mid-life," Paul Tripp says. "All of a sudden, we feel cheated, conned, and stuck. What satisfied us before doesn't do it anymore."[6]

But it's more than just dissatisfaction. It's the death of certain ambitions. It's the burial of our dream.

God uses our lost dreams to achieve his
ambition for us.

It's a fact of life that ambitions get denied. In many cases, some of our long-term dreams are just that—dreams. No one gets all he ever wanted or accomplishes all she set out to do. Our ambitions are strained through the limits of opportunity, of time, of resources, of our own physical capabilities.

It's also a fact of the gospel that denied ambitions are part of God's sovereign plan to direct our lives toward his appointed ends. God uses lost dreams to achieve his ambition for us—that we walk in a manner worthy of our calling.

That's the power that emanates from that great memory verse, Romans 8:28: "And we know that for those who love God *all things* work together for good, for those who are called according to his purpose." The denial of ambitions isn't ultimately a penalty or punishment. It's the gracious work of a loving God defining the path for our walk. He installs fences along the way to keep us moving in his direction. And this expression of God's love isn't limited to midlife.

When ambitions are denied, God's sovereignty is the first thing to go on our internal witness stand. It's not that we change our theology. It's that our theology isn't connected to our unfulfilled desire. We lose sight of God's omniscience and omnipotence. We fail to connect our circumstances with God's goodness. Making that connection can be the difference between delight and disillusionment.

As a college graduate with a criminology degree and police certification, my dream was to get on the local police force. But jobs were scarce and openings rare. We could've moved, but we were in a great church. After several years of shift work as a security guard at the local hospital, I got my shot. Dozens applied, but it came down to me and three other candidates. I knew God was with me, and the door was finally opening. This moment seemed custom-made and hand-delivered for the satisfaction of that dream.

I didn't get the job.

In fact, I never did get a police job. But within a year I relocated to Philadelphia, and a year later, I was in ministry. That was twenty-four years ago. Police work was my dream, and I thought it was God's plan for me. I was ambitious for a good thing, but he had something better planned. God stepped in and fenced in my dream, and I found my call.

God loves us so much he'll intentionally fence us in to keep us on his road. That can be hard, I know. It's never easy to stare at a fence suddenly blocking the path we want to take. But God fences our road to keep us moving in his direction.

Maybe you're wondering how you got here—unemployed, disabled, unhappily married, an unexpected child, a frustrating job. You never thought your road would go in this direction. You've made every attempt, prayed every prayer, read every book—but nothing ever changes.

We find no peace in life until we're convinced our path is his way and our place is his choice. That's so important it's worth repeating: *your place is his choice.* Fences and all.

When God is fencing our ambition, it can sure seem to constrain our freedom. But fences don't simply contain, they protect. A good fence keeps us on the right path and prevents us from hurtling over cliffs, even if it seems we're chasing something good.

Remember, God's agenda for our ambition is about shaping us to use us. God isn't beyond denying certain ambitions to achieve a greater good in us and through us.

It All Leads to Delight

God created ambition because it has the potential to glorify him and delight us.

Ambition is so important that God undertakes a lifelong project in us, forming the ambitions that exalt him and enthuse us. As God moves to the center of our dreams, our desires conform to his glory. God then grants desires because he knows they will magnify his name, not ours. Psalm 37:4 says, "Delight yourself in the LORD, and he will give you the desires of your heart."

As we cooperate with God's work, what delights us is no longer indulged ambition, or even ambitions for God, but God himself.

So let me ask you: What lies at the end of your ambition? Are your goals built around that job you've got to have, the weight you've got to lose, that position in the church with your name on it?

Or are your dreams increasingly built around God and his life-shaping activity in you?

David Sacks wonderfully describes the cumulative impact on life when ambitions are trained by God:

> Every day I'm able to take a picture, it's only because God has enabled me to do that. God has created my senses to see beauty and appreciate it. He's created everything I've ever photographed. I'm

now more open to explore the things that God puts in front of my camera and in my imagination.

I think God wants me to have ambition to be a good photographer. But that's not his primary purpose for me. God wants me to have ambition to be a person who lives for Him in everything.

5

Ambition's Confidence

GOD-CENTERED FAITH SPARKS
GOD-GLORIFYING AMBITION

Did you ever come across a story that walloped you right between the eyes? This one, reported by Tim Stafford in *Christianity Today*, did it for me.

Lalani Jayasinghe lived in the southernmost part of Sri Lanka. Widowed twelve years after her wedding day and living in a simple home with no plumbing, Lalani had few earthly reasons to be joyful and content. But she was a Christian and an active member of her local church.

A few years ago, Lalani was chosen to represent her church for a meeting in the capital city of Colombo to discuss the current challenges Sri Lankan Christians were facing with persecution. Lalani had personal experience with persecution. While at home with her son one day, her husband was brutally killed by local monks hostile to followers of Jesus.

Lalani took the all-day trip to Colombo for the meeting where many churches were gathering for updates, prayer, and support. They wanted to strategize on how to respond to the violence they were facing.

Stafford tells her response:

> When asked how things were with her church, she replied, "Wonderful! Praise the Lord!" Later she gave a more detailed report, telling how the local opposition had that week organized a protest march against her church, and then burned the thatch roof.
>
> Stunned by this news, someone in the meeting asked why she said that everything was wonderful. "Obviously," she answered

enthusiastically, "since the thatch is gone, God must intend to give us a metal roof!"[1]

So let me see if I have this straight: Lalani is a victim of violent persecution. She's already experienced tremendous personal loss, then local mobs burn the roof off her church. Yet her response is praise. Honestly, I don't think I would have come within a mental mile of her interpretation of that event. If a tornado rips the roof off my house tonight, I'll be thinking of insurance, not roof upgrades. But Lalani had her eyes set on something higher. In fact, I have a friend who knows Lalani, and he says that seeing metal roofs when thatched roofs burn is typical of her approach to life.

Why don't I see life that way? What's the big difference between Lalani and me? I think it comes down to one ambition-shaping, risk-taking, life-transforming word.

Faith.

There's a verse in Scripture that hijacked my brain a few years ago and stays there, stubbornly arguing with me anytime a roof catches fire in my life. It's a persistent sentence that defines the difference between Lalani's perspective and the way I so often respond to far less ominous obstacles in my life. Here it is:

> And without faith it is impossible to please him, for whoever would draw near to God must believe that he exists and that he rewards those who seek him. (Heb. 11:6)

You probably noticed this passage is from Hebrews 11, the great faith chapter of the Bible. When I was a kid in Sunday school, they called Hebrews 11 "The Hall of Faith." That was cool, you know, God mixing together baseball and Bible. But Babe Ruth has nothing on the folks in this chapter. Hebrews 11 is filled with regular people displaying aspirations greater than anything you'll see in any hall of fame.

We have the patriarch Abraham, who left everything to obey God; Sarah, a senior citizen who believed God for a child; Moses, who refused the riches of Pharaoh in order to identify with his people; the Israelites, who crossed the Red Sea on dry land—this is wild-crazy-ambitious stuff. Folks just like Lalani. Folks not like me.

People like me need to be rescued from shortsightedness. We need the God-sightedness Lalani has—seeing a life beyond the fire. If our ambitions for God's glory are going to take shape, we need to be rescued from our lack of God-sightings. To help in the rescue, God positions us to extend our hand of faith to lay hold of what we prize. Faith, fully displayed, will lead to a life fully lived.

People like me need to be rescued from shortsightedness.

But there's a kicker. "*Whoever* would draw near to God *must* believe." Whoa, those are some no-nonsense words—"*whoever . . . must . . .*" Does that mean me?

You bet. With the introduction of "whoever," we're all invited to take our place in the Hall of Faith. And with "must," we're buckled in and locked down with no exit options.

Just in case you think there's an escape hatch out of Hebrews 11, consider the verses that guard the front and back of the Hall of Faith:

Hebrews 10:38: "But my righteous one shall live by faith, and if he shrinks back, my soul has no pleasure in him."

Hebrews 12:1: "Therefore, since we are surrounded by so great a cloud of witnesses, let us also lay aside every weight, and sin which clings so closely, and let us run with endurance the race that is set before us."

It appears there's no emergency exit from the Hall of Faith. A life of faith isn't optional. But Hebrews 11:6 doesn't throw us an impossible task and leave us unable to achieve it. This amazing verse actually tells us how faith works in us and through us. Understood rightly, this *is* a doorway for every believer into the place set aside for us in the Hall of Faith. And that's an ambition worth pursuing.

Ambition Finds Its Focus through Faith

What's the focus of faith? The answer to that question can reveal a lot about our theological journey.

I grew up with a traditional church background. For us the

purpose of faith was to . . . well, that's really what Sundays were for. Faith meant religiosity—going to church, obeying commandments (it seemed like there were way more than ten), and getting your morality from Bible stories. It didn't take. Not for me anyway.

I experienced my conversion in college through the influence of some Christians with charismatic leanings. All of a sudden my hands went up whenever I was singing, and faith was a big deal to everybody all the time. Faith was power to do stuff for God, and the world was our laboratory. Sure, God was in there somewhere. But this thing called faith was truly awesome—and it was mine!

A friend of mine wrote a popular song that perfectly captured my grasp on faith in those early years of my Christian life. (I won't mention his name because he now disavows any memory of writing it.)

> I have a destiny I know I shall fulfill;
> I have a destiny in that city on a hill;
> I have a destiny, it's not an empty wish;
> For I know I was born for such a time as this.

I . . . I . . . I . . . I . . . You get the picture. This was my theme song. In my Dave-centered mind, faith was about me and what I was going to do for God.

If there's any upside to that approach, it does kick-start expectations for God to use us. But I don't think this is what Hebrews 11:6 has in view.

Faith isn't some mysterious, detached,
force-like power.
Faith starts with God and fixes on God.

As I began to study God's Word, I fell in love with the doctrines of grace. I discovered these God-centered, Christ-exalting truths in the writings of John Calvin, the Puritans, Jonathan Edwards, and Charles Spurgeon. Those doctrines continue to shape me through the words of contemporaries like J. I. Packer, John Piper, D. A. Carson, and a host of others who inspire me with their words and lives.

In the doctrines of grace I discovered that faith isn't some mysterious, detached, force-like power. Faith starts with God and fixes on God. That's why Hebrews 6:1 calls it "faith toward God." Faith comes from God and is quickened in us because of Christ's death for us.

I know, there's plenty of "faith" teaching going around that instructs people to believe that faith generates its own creative power. But that leads us inward and selfward, not upward and Godward. Our faith doesn't create prosperity, healings, and breakthroughs. Our faith focuses fervently on God. Biblical faith confidently—even ambitiously—asks God to act according to his promises. True faith then accepts the answer. Our faith stands on the unchanging character of God.

Now if you, like me, love all things Reformational, can I have a word with you? I love the confidence and emphasis on God's sovereignty that characterizes the heritage of Luther and the other Reformers and the Puritans and lots of other folks like them. May that never change! But I believe there can be a tendency in our systematic world to allow a theological emphasis on God's sovereignty—which is good and necessary—to wrongly mute a conscious awareness of our need to actively grow in faith. If our understanding of doctrine creates passivity toward God's empowering presence or cools the hot embers of our ambition, we've misunderstood God's sovereignty. When we rightly understand God's caring control over all things, that knowledge should ignite robust faith toward him and bold desire to act in our hearts. We see God more clearly so our ambition can reach further.

So what's the focus of faith in Hebrews 11:6? The writer states it this way: "Whoever would draw near to God . . ." The focus of true faith is not hills to be taken, battles to be won, or trials to be endured. The focus of true faith is God—and not just God in the abstract, theological sense. It's the God who's made known in the person of Jesus Christ.

Jesus announced, "I am the way, and the truth, and the life. No one comes to the Father except through me" (John 14:6). God has given us the desire to draw close to him through the regenerating power of the cross (Titus 3:5). He has revealed himself as our Father through the reconciling mercy of the cross (Gal. 1:3–4). And he has made a way for us to enjoy unhindered access and standing with him in the privileges that come from our justification and adoption as children and co-heirs in Christ (Rom. 5:1–2).

Drawing near to God, then, is not like climbing an endless spiral of steps toward some unknown destination. Drawing near to God is a life of intimate fellowship with a Person, a life of overwhelming wonder that puts everything else into perspective.

If you're wondering what to read during your times with God, I suggest studying the lives of the people profiled in this Hall of Faith. Hebrews 11 gives you the executive summary; go back and read their stories, and you'll get the full drama of people in relationship with God.

Paradoxically, when faith focuses on its main objective—drawing near to God—we don't become religiously obsessed or "too heavenly minded to be any earthly good." We actually get perspective, and we can deal with the complexities and curveballs of life in a balanced way. Consider Charlotte's story.

Charlotte was a single Christian woman who faithfully worked her way up the management ladder of a prominent publishing company. Like many women, she had a constant struggle between two godly but competing ambitions. She had a lifetime desire to be married and raise a family, but it's not as if she could snap her fingers genie-like and make that happen. Charlotte also recognized that God had gifted and promoted her at work and that there were both personal and evangelistic opportunities in her career that marriage and family might change.

Had Charlotte focused on her unfulfilled desire to be married, she might have begun to see her vocation as God's default plan, where second best was as good as it gets, or even a daily reminder of God's lesser care and love for her. At the same time, she never felt able to jettison dreams of marriage and throw herself fully into the corporate world.

Here's how she describes walking the tightrope between the different poles of those ambitions:

> I never wanted to be the president of the company. But I did want to be able to use my gifts in the workplace to be able to support

myself and to be generous to others. I always thought that as long as I was single and responsible for supporting myself, I should do my best to serve the people and corporation God had set me in. I think that attitude led to my career advancement more than any strategic planning for professional advancement.

Still, almost every day was a battle to see God's goodness. I battled serious envy when roommates got married, when coworkers went home to their families, and even when my coworkers' live-in boyfriends and girlfriends stopped by to chat. There were temptations to enter into ungodly relationships with people I met at work. By God's grace, I resisted that kind of relationship, but I sometimes was tempted to think that the price for purity was awfully high!

In my mid to late thirties, I began to envy even the child-care and school problems my coworkers had with their children. As a single woman with no children, who often had to cover for those with sick spouses and kids, I was tempted to wonder what people thought of me. I wondered if they thought about "why" I was single. Did they think no one wanted me or that I was selfishly pursuing some big career? I often felt "different."

The source of much of my envy and discontent was sinful comparison. I hadn't yet learned that God leads each person on his own path, and that to demand to know "Why me?" or "Why not me?" is really questioning God's loving-kindness and faithfulness.

I began to see that money, prestige, charm, and power could be deceitful traps, and that they could disappear in a moment. With God's help, I realized that the only thing I could count on was God himself. I grew (I think) wisely fearful of settling for anything other than a singularly focused, sold-out, proven commitment to God and his purposes.

Though it wasn't easy, Charlotte learned that the answer wasn't putting faith in either marriage or career. It was drawing near to God with a confidence that he would work out his purposes perfectly for her.

I know a number of godly single women who can identify with Charlotte, women who bounce between ambitions for marriage and ambitions for the ministry field of their jobs. For Charlotte, God resolved that tension just before her fortieth birthday, bringing her the husband who was truly the answer to her prayers. How do I know? I work with him, and you won't find a godlier man than my friend Pat.

But Charlotte's need to draw near to God didn't end when her desire for marriage was fulfilled. Charlotte will tell you that drawing near to God by faith is not the way we fulfill our ambitions; it's the only focus worthy of true ambition.

Ambition Battles Unbelief with Faith

The good news in Hebrews 11:6 is that with faith we *can* please God. But this verse gets us there through a double negative: "*without* faith it is *impossible*" to please him.

Why does the author put it this way? He's driving home the point that the normal song of the human heart isn't the song of faith. Although it works out in different ways, Christians and non-Christians share a similar struggle. We both struggle with unbelief.

Unbelief is serious—the writer of Hebrews has already labeled it toxic when he warned us against "an evil heart of unbelief" (3:12, KJV). So we shouldn't get to Hebrews 11 and find a lot of sympathy for unbelief.

The writer there tells us that without faith it's "impossible to please" God. Not tricky, not difficult. No, it's impossible!

I don't think we tend to feel as strongly about unbelief as God does.

Unbelief is a decided distrust in the promises and character of God. Spurgeon describes unbelief as a "mistrust [of] the promises and faithfulness of God."[2] Unbelief denies God's perfections and power and flings his mercies toward sinners back in his face. Unbelief is effectively calling God, if not an outright liar, at least a bait-and-switch artist.

Imagine you have a relationship with some folks to whom you always tell the truth and keep your promises. Your disposition—no matter what, without fail—is to be gracious to them. You're always kind, merciful, helpful, and available at any time.

Now imagine how you'd feel if they frequently doubted you even existed or constantly shrank back from you as if you were about to smack them or were fearful you would repossess everything you'd ever given them, just for spite. Despite your track record, they kept insisting that you just couldn't be trusted. Imagine the affront to your character, the insult to your benevolence, and the assault on your integrity.

Most Christians, beginning with me, rarely see themselves with that kind of bold-faced unbelief. But it happens. A lot.

Sadly, unbelief isn't confined to the big moments of disease and downsizing. Unbelief starts in the little things. We get a bad report on the kids, our plans for the day are interrupted, the stock market drops unexpectedly, and without skipping a beat we're wondering if God is a con artist.

My friends say I have a beautiful mind. I wish they meant I was real smart, like that crazy guy in the book and the movie. But what they really mean is that I sometimes see things that aren't there—like that crazy guy in the book and the movie. Have you ever met anyone like that? Are you like that?

Take, for example, the time someone said to me, "You know what, we really need to talk." My unbelieving mind sprang to life, manufacturing fear-filled scenarios. "Yep, it's bad news, probably some kind of correction. No, he's probably leading a split in the church, and he's been appointed to tell me. No, they've put a contract out on me—he's a hit man!"

Turns out he wanted to tell me how one of my sermons helped him.

Sometimes my mind needs a cage. In fact, I'll let you in on a little secret. Christian mystics in the past used to speak of "the dark night of the soul." For me, it's usually mornings. Most days, as soon as my alarm goes off, my problems magically appear clustered around my bed. They're my Unbelief Ushers, welcoming me to a new day.

"Hey, Dave, we've been waiting for you. We have your day all planned. Let's begin with a good worry workout, followed by a nice long shower of self-pity. We have a yummy breakfast of irresolvable problems all laid out. After that you go right to your past failures rehearsal. The afternoon is dedicated to futility training at your in-box. And we have a great evening of disappointment planned for you, if you make it that far. So let's get up—rise and gloom!"

Oh, and did I mention they're all wearing T-shirts that say "God doesn't exist, or if he does, he doesn't like Dave"? I think they arrive early because they know that's when I'm most likely to agree with them.

Boom—first thing in the morning, before I'm even caffeinated, I have a choice: faith or unbelief.

━━ ━━ ━━ ━━ ━━ ━━ ━━ ━━ ━━ ━━ ━━ ━━ ━━ ━━ ━━ ━━ ━━ ━━ ━━ ━━

First thing in the morning, before I'm even caffeinated, I have a choice: faith or unbelief.

━━ ━━ ━━ ━━ ━━ ━━ ━━ ━━ ━━ ━━ ━━ ━━ ━━ ━━ ━━ ━━ ━━ ━━ ━━ ━━

If unbelief can be that nearby and persistent, it's easy to see how it can become a habit. In fact, as you read through the Bible you'll see that unbelief isn't often an event but a condition. It's a paralysis of soul. When we stumble into unbelief, we tend to stay in the ditch of doubt. We're never truly comfortable there but are unmotivated to do anything about it.

Unbelief chokes godly ambition. If we're gripped by unbelief, life is about survival, and faith is a mirage. All we see is thatched roofs burning. God is nowhere to be found. And the ironic thing is that the only antidote to unbelief is faith.

That's why it's so important to see faith as a gift from God. If faith were from us, when it's vanquished by unbelief, we would have lost it forever. But because faith is a gift coming to me as a benefit of the cross, we can access it by turning to Christ. I think we can all identify with the man who cried out to Jesus, "I believe; help my unbelief!" (Mark 9:24).

We battle unbelief with faith because faith's goal is drawing near to God. The eyes of faith can focus only on the goal of God. There may be a lot of things distracting us, but biblical faith has a singular focus.

Did you ever climb to the top of an old bell tower or church steeple on a spiral staircase—you know, the kind where you look down the center and feel like you're in a Hitchcock movie? If you have a problem with heights, you have a problem with those stairs. So the people who know about such things tell you to look at the steps in front of you or at the back of someone climbing ahead of you—but *don't look down the center.* Why? Because there's nothing to focus on. Just a great expanse of space with certain doom at the bottom.

What happens when you focus upward? You gain confidence to move ahead.

I know someone who learned a lot about faith. Siva grew up as a Brahman Hindu in southern India. After he moved to the United States to pursue higher education, the Lord kindly opened Siva's heart to the gospel, and he was radically converted. Through a long journey filled with many fascinating stories of God's sovereignty, Siva made his way to Philadelphia, married a godly Christian woman, and began to pursue a career in his field of expertise, corrosion engineering.

A few years ago Siva believed God was leading him to start his own engineering firm. This meant, among other things, leaving the comforts of a good job. Siva describes it as "a leap of faith." He'd always wanted to start his own business, but it was a long road.

For six years Siva did everything he could to make the business work. Web site, graphics, cold calls, networking, attending conferences—if there was some way to make connections, Siva was there. But he just couldn't turn the corner. Eventually it became obvious that he needed to close his business and return to work for someone else. If you've ever been in this situation, you can appreciate not only the test of faith but the test of humility that comes by admitting you simply can't make your business work.

But closing his business didn't end Siva's trials. Finding a new job became a trial too. The Lord launched Siva on a faith journey requiring him to stand daily against unbelief. He had to fight doubts about God, doubts about the future, doubts about his ability to provide for his family.

One crucible that emerged was the question of whether to move to another part of the country. Siva believed he was called to raise his family in his local church. But after months of searching, there were simply no jobs in his specialty that would allow him to stay in the area. Siva's options seemed reduced to a painful choice: should he leave the field he'd trained for or leave the church he loved? Siva was trying to do the right thing, but everything else seemed so wrong. Sometimes when he prayed he felt like God was distant and unavailable rather than poised to bless him and keep him.

What does a man do when he doubts whether he's heard from God, whether his future is secure, and whether his ambitions have financially destroyed him?

But Siva had biblical faith—the kind that finds its focus in God, not in ourselves. Siva decided to trust God's Word more than his feelings or his failings. Though there would be no sin in moving his family in order to support them, his biblical convictions caused him to see himself as a man in community more than a man in business. He decided to stay in his local church and take any job he could get.

> What do we do when we doubt whether
> we've heard from God and whether
> our future is secure?

It won't surprise you to discover that God provided a way. It wasn't the greatest job, but it was local. It would also keep him in his field and keep his family in their local church. Siva was willing to sacrifice his own personal vision for the sake of things he valued more.

We'll return to his story later, but let's not miss the key point. Siva had God-centered faith. He didn't run himself into debt trying to keep a dying dream afloat. He didn't compromise his values to solve his problems. And he didn't accuse God when his faith, for a time, seemed to be a fruitless leap. He stood on truth and sought wise counsel. And when doubt came, Siva believed that the God of his conversion and the God of his trial were the same—and could be trusted with both.

Do you find yourself caught in the trap of unbelief? Does God seem distant, preoccupied, unavailable? Have you followed what you thought was God's leading only to find yourself on a difficult road?

Like Siva, refuse to see yourself as a victim of your circumstances. This will free you to take your eyes off your circumstances and fix them on God. Then seek help. But don't ask others for sympathy; ask them for the truth of Scripture. Ask them to remind you who this God is and why he's worthy of your faith. This will help align your thinking with objective truth, not subjective interpretations or emotional thinking. Then confess the sin of unbelief and receive mercy in time of need. This will help you receive the cleansing of forgiveness and fresh faith for a new walk.

Ambition Is Confident in Ultimate Reward

Faith seems like such a noble, almost royal thing, doesn't it? For me, it calls to mind those guards with the tall fuzzy hats in front of the royal palace in England. (Does the queen look out her window and say, "I feel so safe; guys with funny hats are guarding my palace"?) These royal guards are known for absolute devotion to duty. Don't you dare try to get them to smile for a picture, don't try to ask them for directions, and don't ask what's inside their hat. All you get is that rigid-at-attention, eyes-straight-forward, people-without-hats-are-really-odd, God-save-the-Queen kind of look. It's really something to admire.

But Hebrews 11:6 tells us something about faith that goes beyond a single-minded devotion and risk-taking trust in God: *He rewards those who seek him.* John Piper emphasizes that inherent in who God reveals himself to be is what God promises to do: "God is real. God is a rewarder."[3] A significant part of faith is the confidence that God responds to faith.

How crazy is this? God gives us faith as a gift, arranges our circumstances to call it forth, gives us grace to act boldly in faith—then rewards *us* for it! Faith is a work of God for which we are rewarded.

Ambitious faith is always moving forward, persevering, tackling obstacles as they come.

Godly ambition has reward in mind at all times. When our desire for glory is energized by the Hebrews 11 kind of true faith, bold things tend to happen. We do self-denying things the world could never imagine doing. We resist self-indulgence. We take risks for the sake of the gospel. Big risks like proclaiming the gospel in a country where to be a Christian is punishable by death. And little risks like proclaiming the gospel in an office or classroom where to be a Christian is punishable by snickering.

Most of all, ambitious faith is always moving forward, persevering, tackling obstacles as they come, knowing that somewhere out there is promised reward.

My friend Larry is a great example of this persevering ambition.

Larry is a pastor who loves the local church. He loves to care for and help lead the congregation he's a part of, and he loves to be with his family. But since Larry was about six, he dreamed of traveling. The dreams were nurtured by a lot of trips to the airport. "I'd watch my dad walk down the jetway," Larry recalls, "and I thought it was a magic tunnel. I'd imagine all the adventure it held. I'd think, *There's so much adventure out there, and one day I want to do that.*"

As Larry finished high school, his dreams for travel never disappeared, but he dropped out of college and didn't have a lot of direction. He was managing mini-golf courses, did some landscaping on the side, and occasionally painted houses or built decks. It's safe to say that ambition wasn't on his radar screen.

Larry was converted at the age of twenty-one. He was led to the Lord by a friend whose life had been dramatically changed by the gospel. Then Larry met Marilyn, the woman who eventually became his wife. She encouraged Larry toward an active trust in God that brought risk-taking ambition into view. His first major step in ambition was finishing his degree in education. Then they found themselves helping to start a church in the Washington, D.C., area. Larry also found success as a coach of a high school sports team that was nationally ranked.

Larry's dreams to travel hadn't changed, but he increasingly felt the call to ministry, which was confirmed by others. Eventually he took a staff position at his new church and settled into a life of no-travel local church ministry.

In a meeting one day, Larry heard about an upcoming mission trip to India. Because of his long-held dream of travel, he stepped out in faith and humbly expressed his interest in going on the trip. Six months later he found himself on a plane to northern India—his first-ever international trip.

What happened on that trip cemented a remarkable milepost in Larry's life. Larry discovered he didn't simply like to travel. He *loved* going to places the average American would work really hard to avoid.

I've clocked a considerable amount of international travel hours myself, and I can attest, how exhausting it is to spend days on planes, stumble through time zones, eat unfamiliar food, acclimate to radically different cultures, bang up against impenetrable language barriers, and devote every waking hour to doing ministry. Travel leaves me wrung out for days. But Larry has an unusual grace on his life. Difficult travel and challenging cross-cultural ministry actually energize him. When he's hauling his suitcase off the baggage claim, he's mentally and emotionally ready to jump on another plane and head to the next remote gospel outpost. And Marilyn, who never wanted to marry a pastor or leave the D.C. suburbs, loves the work God has given Larry to do.

The call on Larry's life to this "sent" ministry has been so pronounced that others in ministry thought it wise to position him in a larger church where his travel wouldn't conflict with the needs of the local congregation. Today ambitionless Larry is ambassador Larry. But to get there, he faithfully served where he was, trusted God with his ambition . . . and patiently waited.

It was twenty-two years after Larry became a Christian before God finally allowed him to travel. During that time, Larry says, "God showed me my selfish ambition. For all those years, my ambition for travel was rooted in my own desires." Now, Larry says, "Every time I get on a plane, I shake my head and think *I can't believe I get to do this.*"

Selfish ambition would insist, "I have a right to do this. I need it. This fulfills me." Ambition rooted in God says, "I *don't* need it; instead I'll serve wherever and however I can. This glorifies God."

Larry has it right—his ambitions are Godward. They recognize that God is real and that God is a rewarder.

Larry also knows that life won't always be like this. As with all of us, eventually a younger guy will come along and take his place. "Just let me know when you want me to step aside," Larry says. "I'll do it for as long as I'm needed, but not a minute more." Here's a man who has finally received the desire of his heart after years of patient and godly perseverance. And now he's willing to let it go. Why? Is it no longer fulfilling for him? Is he looking for the next step up the ministry ladder? Is he burned out?

No! Larry received a reward for his faith, but he's looking to a reward that's well beyond what he does in this life. He's finding his own little place in the Hall of Faith, like saints before him, assured of things hoped for, convinced of things not seen. Traveling around the world in the service of the gospel? Yes, that's a reward. But it's not the ultimate reward. That's something we haven't yet seen—but it's unimaginably good.

Remember Siva? He faced failure and went back to work for somebody else. What Siva didn't factor in was that God was going to use that job to create some significant avenues for him to begin to specialize in a field of his industry that was just about to explode.

In a remarkable "coincidence," Siva's employer made the business decision to move away from this specialty, requiring them to cut Siva loose from his employment and forcing him to restart his company— just when this area of his field was demanding his unique expertise. At a time of economic downturn, but with years of contracted work ahead of him, Siva is hard at work trying to keep up with the demands of his business. His business has quickly quadrupled. But he knows that none of this has come from his efforts. Success, after persevering through failure, is evidence of God rewarding those who seek him.

What about Charlotte? Well, she finds herself in her mid-forties and the mother to three small children. In the natural realm, that wasn't supposed to happen. But it has, because God is a rewarder of those who seek him.

Not All Happy Endings—for Now

Hebrews 11 makes it clear that not every story of faith has a happy ending—at least not the earthly chapter of the story.

Even though Lalani believed, her husband died at the hands of persecutors, her son grew up without a father, and her church was set on fire. But her faith was set to see the Savior, and she looked back at God's faithfulness and found joy because she believed that God is real and that he's a rewarder of those who seek him.

There's no way we'll receive in this life all the reward for our faith. The truth is, our life on this side of heaven can't hold all the reward. It's stored up for us not because we need to be patient, but because it's so magnificent we couldn't handle it here.

That's why you'll find folks like Lalani in the part of the Hall of Faith with this plaque over the door:

These all died in faith, *not having received the things promised*, but having seen them and greeted them from afar, and having acknowledged that they were strangers and exiles on the earth. For people who speak thus make it clear that they are seeking a homeland. If they had been thinking of that land from which they had gone out, they would have had opportunity to return. But as it is, they desire a better country, that is, a heavenly one. Therefore God is not ashamed to be called their God, for he has prepared for them a city. (Heb. 11:13–16)

That's the fitting inscription as well for most of the people who instruct us from church history down through the centuries. Meanwhile, folks like Larry, Siva, and Charlotte still have other ambitions and dreams that may or may not be rewarded in this life.

Godly ambition finds its focus through faith. It battles unbelief with faith. It leans on faith when circumstances scream otherwise. And ambition is confident in the ultimate reward.

6

Ambition's Path

THE PATH OF AMBITION IS A PARADOX

Maybe you've heard the story of the violinist performing in a Metro station in Washington, D.C. Of course, street musicians play for money in subways all the time. But this guy was no street musician, and he certainly didn't need the money.

His name is Joshua Bell, a Grammy award-winning, world-renowned violinist. He was also playing a Stradivarius violin worth $3.5 million—the 1713 Gibson ex-Huberman Stradivarius, to be precise. (I have no idea what that means, but just typing the name impresses me.)

The Washington Post tapped Mr. Bell to conduct an experiment. They dressed Joshua in humble garb—blue jeans, casual shirt, and ball cap. Then they had him perform some of the most difficult compositions possible. (In case your mind works like mine, "The Devil Went Down to Georgia" was not on the list.)

Master violinist Bell played for about forty minutes. During that time, more than eleven hundred people passed by. Only seven stopped to listen. The video footage shows that at the conclusion of each piece, there was no applause, no accolades—just the sound of subway trains whistling toward destinations around the city. Reflecting on the experience, Mr. Bell commented, "It was a strange feeling that people were . . . um . . . ignoring me!"[1]

The *Post* called it "a test of people's perceptions and priorities."[2] Would people perceive the presence of an authentic violin master? Would they notice? Would they make it a priority to listen?

They didn't. I don't blame them. Violin masters aren't found in subways wearing blue jeans and ball caps. For that you need $200 and the Kennedy Center stage. After all, if you're not dressed like a master or performing where masters play, you're probably just another schmuck like the rest of us, right?

The Master in Disguise

The New Testament brings us before another Master. No ball cap, no violin, but he crossed a wider gap than a master in the Metro. Wrapped in the rags of humanity, Jesus Christ came to subway earth. "The Word became flesh and dwelt among us" (John 1:14). It was the ultimate test in perception and priorities. One performance only.

The Son of God come to earth! What would the reviewers talk about after he left the theater? Amazing power? Yes, and plenty of it. Incredible wisdom? Mind-boggling. Exemplary character? Perfect. But what's the most remarkable thing about this performance?

One word. *Humility.*

Consider what the apostle Paul points us to when he reminds us of Jesus on the stage of human history.

> Do nothing from rivalry or conceit, but in humility count others more significant than yourselves. Let each of you look not only to his own interests, but also to the interests of others. Have this mind among yourselves, which is yours in Christ Jesus, who, though he was in the form of God, did not count equality with God a thing to be grasped, but made himself nothing, taking the form of a servant, being born in the likeness of men. And being found in human form, he humbled himself by becoming obedient to the point of death, even death on a cross. (Phil. 2:3–8)

This passage is part of a letter to a church Paul loved. He celebrates his partnership with them (1:3–5, 8) and prays for them (1:9). The advance of the gospel among them is ever foremost in his mind (1:5, 27). But like all churches, Philippi has its share of colorful personalities and problems. Later, in chapter 4, Paul mentions two ladies, Euodia and Syntyche, who seem to have public disagreements. Their conflict seems typical of a broader disunity within the church. Selfish ambition is working its divisive magic, as it never fails to do.

So in the style of *The Washington Post*, Paul engages in his own "test of perception and priorities." But he's testing much more than musical taste in those words quoted above from Philippians 2. Commentator F. B. Meyer called this passage "almost unapproachable in its unexampled majesty."

Unexampled majesty . . . in *humility*. It seems like a contradiction, doesn't it? Or at least a paradox. Paul is, in fact, pointing us to perhaps *the* greatest paradox ever: God almighty in humility. The path of humility is the path the Son of God took to reach us. And, as we'll see, the greatest ambitions are realized paradoxically on the path of humility.

Paradox One:
The Greatest Fulfillment Is Found in Emptiness

Paul isn't giving the Philippians a pop quiz in theology. This is a road test of what it means to live in light of the gospel. Imitation is more than the sincerest form of flattery; Paul indicates that it's vital to our call as Christians. "Have this mind among yourselves, which is yours in Christ Jesus," he says (2:5). Imitate the mind of Christ; adopt the Master's mind-set.

If you're wondering what that means, Paul doesn't leave us speculating:

> [Christ Jesus], though he was in the form of God, did not count equality with God a thing to be grasped, but made himself nothing, taking the form of a servant, being born in the likeness of men. And being found in human form, he humbled himself by becoming obedient to the point of death, even death on a cross. (2:6–8)

He was *in the form of God*? Is that like a God-wannabe? Christ "in the form of God," but not God himself? Is it like my buddy who has a twin brother? Or like, "Wow, did anybody ever tell you that you look like . . . ?" God's duplicate copy, but not the real thing?

No, not at all.

The Greek word for "form" deals with the essential character or nature of something—same rank, status, or station in existence.[3] Paul is saying that the pre-incarnate Jesus existed as God. Make no mistake, Christ is equal to God; he is coequal, coeternal, same essence, the works. The Nicene Creed says that Jesus is "very God of very God." That's a cool, creedal way to say he was *GOD*—accept no substitutes.

But what Paul says next really blows our theological gaskets. Although Jesus was wholly God, he "did not count equality with God a thing to be grasped." Though he shared the rights, honors, and privileges of God, Jesus didn't selfishly protect his position or prestige but gave them up—ultimately to die on the cross for our sins.

We're called to a radical humility expressed most clearly in the temporary, voluntary self-emptying of the Son of God himself.

The impulse to stop right here and fall on our knees in worship for the saving grace of God in Christ is almost overwhelming. But as we worship, let's follow the application Paul is making to the Philippians. He's calling us to a radical humility expressed most clearly in the temporary, voluntary self-emptying[4] of the Son of God himself.

See the irony here? People seek their fulfillment in the things they acquire or earn. Jesus shared in the glory of God, and he gave that up. Jesus wasn't just the exceptionally gifted guy in the class who aced every test and dominated every spelling bee. No, when galaxies a million light-years away were spoken into existence, Jesus was present and working. But he emptied himself of the privileges and prerogatives of deity to become man—to live under our limits and rules. The gospel reminds us that Christ was cosmically downsized to come and die for us. He was really something, but he made himself nothing.

Joshua Bell in a subway station doesn't begin to compare with that.

So what does this mean for us and our ambitions? It means if we want to find true fulfillment in life, we must follow the path of the Master. Whether we're burning with passion for a goal or lacking ambition and don't know where to start, we follow the Savior *downward*.

When we empty ourselves of personal glory, we won't be empty; we'll learn the fullness of Christ. And our ambitions are rescued in the process.

Paradox Two:
It's Wrong to Think First about Rights

"Not count[ing] equality . . . a thing to be grasped" is a phrase that sings to the soul. It sounds great during our morning devotions, and it preaches great at a Bible study. It doesn't become audacious until we're called to actually apply it.

Another car zooms into our parking space while we're sitting patiently with the turn signal on. You did most of the work—someone else got all the credit. You're overlooked again for the ministry position you seem perfectly gifted to do. It's a long list. Are you like me—thinking first of your rights each time you feel wronged?

It doesn't take much for me to realize that holding on to pride gets in the way of humility. But my *rights*? Now you're getting a little pushy, Paul. Everybody knows that equality is a good thing, right? And doesn't equality mean we have to protect our rights? After all, it's a dog-eat-dog world out there. And I have rights, inalienable rights if I read the Declaration of Independence correctly. And don't forget that little thing called the Bill of Rights. So hey, buddy, back off my rights!

Who had greater rights than Jesus?
But he gave those up in order to gain our salvation.

But who had greater rights than Jesus? He had equality with God—the right to be worshiped by every created thing and the rights of full authority and power over them all. But he gave those up in order to gain our salvation.

It's not that rights don't matter. They do. When one person violates the rights of another, that's injustice and oppression. But while we want to be known as defenders of the legitimate rights of others, we aren't supposed to be known by our ambition to protect our personal rights. To follow Christ means to see allegiance to him as more significant than any right we hold in this life. To be faithful to Christ, we'll have to give up rights—perhaps even our right to our own lives.

With their faithfulness to the Savior, my persecuted brothers and sisters around the world remind me that we live by grace, not by rights. To be a Christian is to recognize that the only thing we have a perfect right to is the wrath of God—and that's not a right we want to insist on keeping.

A. W. Tozer describes the danger of a "my rights" mentality among Christians:

> Few sights are more depressing than that of a professed Christian defending his supposed rights and bitterly resisting any attempt to violate them. Such a Christian has never accepted the way of the cross. The sweet graces of meekness and humility are unknown to him. He grows every day harder and more acrimonious as he defends his reputation, his rights, his ministry, against his imagined foes.[5]

Being ambitious to move downward confronts how we view our own rights. With Christ and his example ever before us, our view should be distinctly different from the rest of human civilization.

Look at how this worked out in Otto's life.

With ten years of leading worship under his belt, Otto could spot a natural. And the new guy up last Sunday was born to lead worship. However, leading worship was Otto's role in the church, one in which he'd served faithfully, tirelessly, and prayerfully. Yet after praying over it and consulting some friends, he approached his pastor and recommended that the new guy replace him. Why would he orchestrate his own demotion? Because his ambition for Christ was higher than his ambition for any particular role.

It may sound like Alice in Wonderland, but stories like Otto's don't just happen in fairy tales. They happen anywhere ambitions for Christ exceed ambitions for self.

God is at work in the heart of his children, replacing our preoccupation for equality comparisons with an aspiration to empty ourselves. In the Master's realm it's only right that it should be this way.

Paradox Three:
It's Really Something to Be Nothing

Christ could have come as emperor, and no one could have disputed his rightful claim. He deserved the highest position available on earth. In fact, we should have created one—Master of the Universe!—just to accommodate him.

But that's not the position he wanted. He chose another. He took "the form of a servant" (Phil. 2:7).

Servant is an amazing word when applied to God, but it only begins to capture the scope of sacrifice contained in the Greek word here, *doulos*. Perhaps the most accurate translation is "bondslave"— one who voluntarily puts himself in slavery to another.

I know that's provocative, but it's Scripture. God intentionally chose this metaphor to underscore the all-encompassing claim the gospel makes upon our lives. Biblical scholar Murray Harris describes the idea behind this term as it's applied in the New Testament:

> In a fundamental sense slavery involves the absence of rights, especially the right to determine the course of one's life and the use of one's energies. What is denied the slave is freedom of action and freedom of movement; he cannot do what he wishes or go where he wishes. The faculty of free choice and the power of refusal are denied to him.[6]

Are you ambitious for slavery?

The career path for the Christian looks different than for others. We should not be hungry for our own name or unrestrained in our self-promotion. We don't need to broker our future. The gospel reminds us that our ambition should follow Christ's action. If God submitted his great majesty to the call of servanthood, we can submit our musical talents, our teaching desires, our motivational skills to the call of servanthood as well.

How often do we live unsatisfied lives because our positions don't live up to our ambitions? So we grumble at the watercooler or whine in the confines of our car, frustrated because that next logical step is blocked by something or someone.

One great measure of our humility is whether we can be ambitious for someone else's agenda. Not just tolerate and accommodate the goals of those over us, but adopt their vision, promote and pursue their dreams. Our willingness to make others a success is a great measure of the purity of our ambitions.

Our willingness to make others a success is a great measure of the purity of our ambitions.

And believe me, that can look pretty radical. For instance, in a society obsessed with rights and equality, the traditional role of wife and mother—that of helper to the husband, invested in the family—has taken a bad rap. In the world's eye, sacrificing dreams of income, travel, or social status in the service of family seems antiquated, unenlightened, almost Leave-It-To-Beaverish. But to empty oneself in service of a family is an arresting illustration of the Savior's heart and life. I should know. I see it every day in my wife.

Everyone who names Christ as Savior is called to be a servant. Writing to the Philippians, Paul sets up this kind of ambition for others by a call away from "rivalry or conceit" (2:3). "Rivalry" translates the same Greek word that in James is rendered as "selfish ambition" (3:16). Paul's intent is clear. We're to "do nothing" to compete with or usurp others, particularly those over us.

Rivalry is what happens when ambitions swell with envy. Someone else is enjoying what we want for ourselves. Envy burns, and it overshadows our many blessings. We don't have the position, finances, possessions, or gifting of another, so we begrudge them and charge God with inequality. Pretty serious stuff—and a far cry from emptying self and considering others better.

King Saul is the biblical poster child for rivalry. The Scriptures tell us he started out small in his own eyes (1 Sam. 10:20–24). When the prophet Samuel went to anoint him as king, he was hidden among the baggage, probably where he belonged.

But once he was king, envy stalked and captured him. Saul began to resent David, the young man who would replace him. This opened the door to suspicion and judgment. Saul began to ascribe evil motives to David. He went from loving David to despising him. Note that he didn't despise David as a person; he despised him as a rival. The fact of David's being in Saul's life exposed Saul's ambitions: he wasn't serving the people but was protecting his power. David became a threat to his future aspirations, so David had to die. Saul, who was supposed to be a benevolent king, launched a manhunt for one of his subjects.

C. S. Lewis got to the nub of envy's comparative tyranny:

> Ambition! We must be careful what we mean by it. If it means the desire to get ahead of other people . . . then it is bad. If it means simply wanting to do a thing well, then it is good. It isn't wrong for an actor to want to act his part as well as it can possibly be acted, but the wish to have his name in bigger type than the other actors is a bad one. . . . What we call "ambition" usually means the wish to be more conspicuous or more successful than someone else. It is this competitive element in it that is bad. It is perfectly reasonable to want to dance well or to look nice. But when the dominant wish is to dance better or look nicer than the others—when you begin to feel that if the others danced as well as you or looked as nice as you, that would take all the fun out of it—then you are going wrong.[7]

Saul went wrong. His ambition betrayed him. Promising him satisfaction, it turned and destroyed him. On a battlefield overrun by his enemies, Saul committed suicide by falling on his own sword.

Rivalry destroys friendships, splits churches, undermines testimonies, and makes us look no different than the world around us.

The average Christian's experience with rivalry won't end with a person impaled on his own sword. But rivalry does destroy friendships, split churches, undermine testimonies, and make us look no different than the world around us.

Rivalry is serious. Its nature is to subordinate others' interests and to go to irrational lengths to protect our own interests. It's an impulse that we're called and empowered to deny, put off, crucify, kill.

But that isn't the end of Paul's call. Humility counts others more significant than ourselves—it looks out for the interests of others. It's interesting, isn't it, how hard it is to be envious of others' interests when we're actually looking out for them? Humility sees in servant-hood the pathway toward liberation. The gospel-based power of an ambition for others expels the envy and selfish ambition from our lives. We can serve others. We can be second and satisfied.

The instinctive temptation here is to color ourselves outside the lines. "You don't know my situation," you might be thinking. "You don't understand my husband, my boss, my parents, my administrator, my teacher. Their interest is already their top concern. They don't need my help in that department!"

But remember, it's Christ's example that's being held out for us here. He came to those who were enemies of God. He loved those who denied him. He served those who rejected him. He even died for those hostile toward him. When we consider what Christ accomplished, serving our selfish teen or unjust boss seems mundane in comparison.

Never underestimate the unique work that God does in our lives by placing us under unthinking or unscrupulous people. They may appear to hold the joystick on your life. But "the king's heart is a stream of water in the hand of the LORD; he turns it wherever he will" (Prov. 21:1).

Few things root out self-love more than the daily drill of serving others who seem to delight in treating you like a slave. God intentionally creates opportunities where we must serve others, because it rescues our ambitions and forces him to the center. Living for the success of others—that's right, even them—is a wonderful gospel aroma that pleases God. "The greatest among you shall be your servant," Jesus said. "Whoever exalts himself will be humbled, and whoever humbles himself will be exalted" (Matt. 23:11–12).

Rescued ambition no longer clamors to be first or best. It's happy with the comparative nothingness of slavery or second best, if that's what brings the most glory to God.

It really is something to become nothing. Take that to the office, and it will drop some jaws.

Paradox Four:
When It Comes to Self-Evaluation,
Don't Trust What You See

Sometimes we can read these words about looking to others' interests and counting others more significant than ourselves and think, *Okay, all I have to do is just stop thinking about me*. But that isn't what Paul is talking about. Counting others as more significant than ourselves assumes that at some point we're giving thought to ourselves.

Paul clearly links our ability to act in humility with an awareness of our own interests; we're just not to look *only* to our own interests. Elsewhere he instructs the believer not to think of himself more highly than he ought to think, but to "think with sober judgment, each according to the measure of faith that God has assigned" (Rom. 12:3). So according to Paul, the problem for Christians isn't self-awareness; rather, it's the wrong *kind* of self-awareness. The key is a self-awareness based in humility—seeing ourselves with both faith and sober judgment, then living as if others are more significant than we are.

We desperately need the eyes and words of others
to help us form a humble self-perception.

Do you know what I've found? Ambition and self-assessment are inextricably linked. The selfishly ambitious are terrible at self-arithmetic. When they "count themselves," it's always more than almost everybody else. When I live in my house or my church as King Dave, I become blind to my faults and limits. This is why I desperately need the eyes and words of others to help me form a humble self-perception.

The Roman philosopher Seneca once said, "Mirrors were discovered in order that man might come to know himself."[8] I'm not a big fan of mirrors because I often don't like what I see. Have you noticed that most mirrors don't show your whole body? Good or bad, we only see our front. We could be walking around for years with a giant "kick me" sign pasted on our back and never know it.

I'm guessing you don't have a sign on your back. But there are probably some things about you that your friends are aware of but you're not. God has designed us so that we need each other to get a complete picture. We don't learn wisdom in a book or on a mountaintop. Without help from others, we're often blind to what we do and why we do it. We learn wisdom in community. If we stand alone, we fall. That's why humility looks for mirrors. The humble don't just tolerate input; they seek it.

Do you have mirrors in your life? If not, get some. You won't regret it. If you're wondering how they help, here's a few ways they serve me.

MIRRORS HELP WITH MOTIVES

Maybe you've had the experience of cruising along in life or work or ministry, thinking you're doing fine, and then someone drops this little bomb into your productivity parade: "Why?" As in, "Why did you do that, Dave?" Or "Why did you say that, Dave?" Or, more to the point, "What was motivating you, Dave?"

Give me a "what" question any day. I don't mind so much when people question what I do—hey, I'm not perfect, everybody makes mistakes. It's the "why" inquiries that get under my skin.

In God's view, the result isn't the only thing that matters. Motives matter. A lot. So let me ask you: Is there anyone in your life who's free to ask you the "why" questions? And what happens when someone questions your motives for the "good" things you're doing?

If we're doing something good, we maintain the idea that our motives are somehow above question. But there may be no better place to hide selfish motivations than in service to others, even in the church. Service is certainly self-giving, but it can also be tailor-made for cloaking selfish ambition. In fact, I think a lot of divisions in churches happen because folks aren't willing to have their motives questioned. They'll argue fine points of theology, ecclesiology, missiology, pneumatology—all kinds of "ologies"—but they never put on the table a very simple question: "Why does this matter to me so much?"

This also comes into play in what we say. Our world loves conversation. We love to talk about ideas, art, culture, life—bring it on!

Conversation is cool. I love it myself. But sometimes we want to converse about ideas and life as if our talk is disconnected from our heart. We unsuspectingly do what Scripture never permits—we detach our motives from our mouth, forgetting that "out of the abundance of the heart the mouth speaks" (Matt. 12:34).

Unknowingly, we end up in a dangerous place. When our inner world isn't open to scrutiny, our outer world eventually collapses.

If you ever find yourself insisting your motives are unpolluted—*Maybe what I said wasn't right, but my motives were pure*—get out of the shadows and back to your Bible. God's love is so vast that he takes great interest in every aspect of the reasons behind everything we do. One of the ways he shows this remarkable love is by giving us mirrors for our motives.

Let me tell you about something I've done that's difficult for me. I've cracked open the window of evaluation to the level of motives. Yep, I'm talking speech, action, the whole shebang. It was simple but a little hairy to tell my wife, kids, and friends that I want this degree of help. Why do I want it? Because motives matter. My only link to biblical reality is to keep "why" in the picture.

MIRRORS HELP WITH GIFTS

Misha is destined for greatness. At least that's what her parents always told her. Her singing voice peaked early, and by tenth grade she was a regular performer at school. Doors flew open in many churches. But greatness is a reluctant patron, and her ascent stalled. Now in her twenties, she just doesn't understand. "My dream was simple," she says. "I just wanted to use my gifts to serve God." But for Misha, serving God really meant recording contracts and touring. "Why can't people recognize my gifts?" she asks.

Misha has ambitions that seem godly, at least to her. She says she wants to use her gifts "in the service of God." Her friends at church think she's gifted, yes, but probably reaching too high. They're reluctant to talk to her, though, since they know they would discourage her dream.

Imagine you're Misha's friend. What does Misha need? Everybody cheering her on? Or somebody courageous enough to wisely question the dream through some objective assessment? Awkward situation, huh?

Wherever there's a gift, there's a limit.

Misha's story is pretty common, especially in the church. There are Misha musicians, Misha songwriters, Misha preachers, Misha evangelists. Mishas are all around us—and sometimes within us. One of the undeniable realities of spiritual experience is this: *Wherever there's a gift, there's a limit.*

That's why, even if our motives are godly, we all need the mirror of a thoughtful, gracious, but realistic assessment of our gifts from those who know and love us. We need others to help us think of ourselves "with sober judgment" (Rom. 12:3).

What I've found is that recognizing the limits of my gifts actually frees me of the head-banging burden of trying to do something God hasn't intended for me. It also allows me to appreciate the diversity of gifts God has placed around me. God gives us gifts so we can serve others. We discover and refine them in community, not alone in the desert under a cactus. In talking about the church, Paul says, "The eye cannot say to the hand, 'I have no need of you,' nor again the head to the feet, 'I have no need of you'" (1 Cor. 12:21). God makes it clear: we need each other!

The sooner we get this, the easier life becomes. But it can take a while, especially for us men. Permit me to let you in on a little gender secret. While women have two X chromosomes, men have one X, one Y, and one "I-would-rather-drive-into-another-time-zone-than-ask-for-directions" chromosome. This extra chromosome is so dominant that a guy can be three states past his exit and still be looking for the shortcut. That kind of behavior is so irrational it has to be genetic. Men are the only creatures ever known to get in an argument with a GPS. Highways around the world are littered with these devices hurled from the window by men who claim it is obviously malfunctioning.

But it's not really genetics at all. There's something in my heart that doesn't want outside help. It's that inner fool that so often wants to come out and play. To ask for help is a sign that I'm lost, needy, wrong, and desperate—things that are all true, but I would rather lose a lung than admit it. In the moment, driving until we run out of gas seems so much more appealing. But asking for help is better and more biblical.

Grace never comes to the proud. It comes when we humble ourselves and ask for the help we need. We need mirrors to function fruitfully.

Are you Misha? If we want to stir an ambition, let's aspire to truly know who we are and how we might serve best through our gifts. And for that we need others' help.

MIRRORS HELP WITH FRUIT

Hungering for help to determine where I'm gifted and limited, or where I need to be mindful of my motives, is a great start but a poor ending. Rescuing ambition includes evaluating how our efforts are bearing fruit.

Fruitfulness is something that Christ is dead-on serious about. "By this my Father is glorified, that you bear much fruit and so prove to be my disciples" (John 15:8). In other words, God wants our godly efforts to be effective. If this is a main proof that we're disciples, we should aspire to evaluate our effectiveness. Often.

Christians are a funny lot. We're ambitious to start things but hate to end them. Every initiative can seem right, good, and impor-tant—we're sure God is behind it all. So we launch things as if great efforts in the name of God need no expiration dates. We assume that what's effective in one season is effective for all time. Methods become monuments.

We're not the first to face this challenge. The very earliest church faced a similar defining moment. In an extraordinary display of gos-pel leadership, the twelve apostles were personally involved in making sure the widows in the church had food each day. But this created a problem. By giving themselves to the widows, they were neglecting the greater fruitfulness of preaching God's Word. And the church was growing so fast that some widows were being overlooked in the daily food distribution.

The church leaders actually had to sit down and evaluate whether preaching would be more fruitful than serving widows. Oh, man—any pastor worth his salt knows you don't mess with widows. When they pray, God listens! Diss a widow, and you get called down to God's office really quickly. Should the apostles' "fruit inspection" really include evaluating their role with this group?

You'd better believe it. The twelve apostles concluded, "It is not right that we should give up preaching the word of God to serve tables" (Acts 6:2). The fruitfulness of the entire church was at stake, so dramatic action was needed. Serving the widows was a good thing, but the Twelve needed to give themselves to the labors that would bear the most fruit for the most people. So the church had to get radical. Ministry strategies changed for continued care of the widows, new leaders were appointed, the twelve were freed up to focus on preaching and prayer, new ministries started—all to nurture and protect the fruitfulness of the church.

It seemed to work. "And the word of God continued to increase, and the number of disciples multiplied greatly in Jerusalem, and a great many of the priests became obedient to the faith" (6:7).

Someone had the courage to evaluate the widows' real needs. As a result, the church was positioned for growth. An era ended, but a new kind of fruitfulness began.

A good mirror asks unpopular questions about fruit in every season.

A good mirror asks unpopular, even scandalous, questions about fruit in every season. That's not harsh or unkind. It's an important way of knowing whether we should continue or change what we're doing. Mirrors help protect us from two dangerous extremes of ambition: building monuments to our abilities and flaming out in wasted effort.

I'm so grateful for times my friends come in and ask the obvious "why" questions. We've torn down some pretty big monuments over time. And you know what? Nobody seems to care that they're gone.

But this doesn't mean ambition is only a live-in-the-moment thing. A biblical ambition for fruitfulness takes the long view of life. "Burning out" for God may sound radical, but it doesn't position us to bear "much" fruit (John 15:8). We should think about burning long, like the Olympic torch that must travel through many lands before it reaches the final destination. Christians should be ambitious to run long and finish strong.

I cut my Christian teeth on the passion of Keith Green. His zeal for God catalyzed many young believers toward fervor for Christ. Once he said, "I repent of ever having recorded one single song, and ever having performed one concert, if my music, and more importantly my life, has not provoked you into godly jealousy or to sell out more completely to Jesus!"[9] I loved that stuff. "Let's sell out for Jesus; preach it, Keith!" But Keith Green died in a tragic accident at age twenty-nine.

Or there's Jim Elliot, who invested his life in reaching the Huaorani Indians in Ecuador. One can't hear his name without thinking of his famous quote, "He is no fool who gives what he cannot keep to gain that which he cannot lose."[10] This hero also died at twenty-nine, martyred by those he was attempting to reach.

I can't tell you how much I admire the fire, sacrifices, and passion of these men. They burned bright and strong during their sojourn on earth. But most Christians don't die in their twenties. Like Christian journeying toward the Heavenly City in *Pilgrim's Progress*, we walk a longer road where fruitfulness must come and remain over many seasons of life. Make no mistake—God does call us to be sold out for Jesus. But it's a passion spread over a lifetime. It's a journey on which we must press forward through weakness, discouragement, and sin. For the average Joe or Jane, there'll be no book commemorating battles or marking victories.

What is it that sustains fruitfulness, as the old hymn "Amazing Grace" says, "through many dangers, toils and snares"?

The gospel is our only answer. As we daily contemplate our Savior's life, death, and resurrection, we grow more astounded by his unconditional choice before time began.

But his choice carries a call. We must cultivate ambitions to bear fruit for his name.

Rescuing Ambition

Here's the arrangement: *we* aspire to bear fruit; *he* makes sure it remains. "You did not choose me," he says, "but I chose you and appointed you that you should go and bear fruit and that your fruit should abide" (John 15:16).

A strong start is a great start. But finishing strong is the goal. And it is the faithful mirror work of those who evaluate fruit that helps us finish strong. We desperately need to see the goal. And we need the mirrors to help us see our fruit, our gifts, and our motives that are indispensable in the rescue of our ambitions.

Paradox Five: True Humility Promotes Great Ambition

Sometimes we misunderstand humility, assuming that it works against godly ambition. It can strike us as proud to dream about how we might work for God's glory.

But in Philippians 2, Christ's humility is displayed in his action. He "made himself nothing," he took "the form of a servant," "he humbled himself by becoming obedient." To "have this mind among yourselves," as verse 5 instructs us, is to follow an example of action, intention, and initiative. Christ's humility didn't restrain his enterprise; it defined it.

God calls us to follow this example—to be "*zealous* for good works" (Titus 2:14).

> When we become too humble to aspire,
> we've stopped being humble.

Humility is not a fabric softener on our aspirations—smoothing, softening, and tempering our dreams to the point where we're too modest to reach for anything. G. K. Chesterton warned against finding "humility in the wrong place." He appealed for a return to the "old humility," saying,

> The old humility was a spur that prevented a man from stopping; not a nail in his boot that prevented him from going on. For the old

humility made a man doubtful about his efforts, which might make him work harder. But the new humility makes a man doubtful about his aims, which will make him stop working altogether.[11]

When we become too humble to aspire, we've stopped being humble.

Humility should never be an excuse for inactivity. Our humility should harness our ambition, not hinder it. Talking about your dreams for God isn't proud—it's essential. If you're too humble to dream, maybe you have an incorrect understanding of humility. The servant who is faithful with little still has an eye on the much. John Stott has it right:

> Ambitions for self may be quite modest. . . . Ambitions for God, however, if they are to be worthy, can never be modest. There is something inherently inappropriate about cherishing small ambitions for God. How can we ever be content that he should acquire just a little more honour in the world? No. Once we are clear that God is King, then we long to see him crowned with glory and honour, and accorded his true place, which is the supreme place. We become ambitious for the spread of his kingdom and righteousness everywhere.[12]

Are you getting the picture? The stoking of godly ambition is far from inconsequential. Without it, exploration dies, research stops, kids spoil, industry stalls, causes fail, civilizations crumble, the gospel stands still. We can't let all of that happen in the name of humility. If our ambitions are worthy of God's glory, they can never be modest.

To allow such passivity is to cut out the very heart of humility, leaving it devoid of the power and grace God promises to the humble. The "old" humility, true and biblical humility, has a name big enough for the largest of godly ambitions. We must be ambitious for this kind of humility.

Our Path Is Lit

Christians are flammable. God created us to burn. Not like a match, either—bright and hot but quickly extinguished. That does little good for others and brings little glory to God. Ambitions are like a blowtorch. God ignites them, he points them in the right direction, and eternal work gets done. The flame is sustained by the fuel of grace. God's work in God's way for God's glory. Why burn for anything else?

Most people think of ambition as climbing, upward mobility, always looking for a step up (and willing to step on others to get it). But biblical ambition points in the other direction—the direction Christ traveled. Our Master emptied himself, lighting the path for our ambitions. We're called to follow him.

As we empty ourselves, we find the fullness of Christ. We look out for others' rights ahead of our own. We find joy in advancing others' success. We ask others to help us think realistically about ourselves. We follow Christ, who was in the form of God but made himself nothing.

It's a paradox: Godly ambition makes us *downwardly* mobile. Whether we see the implications of this call is a far better test of perception and priorities than any master violinist in the Metro.

Godly ambitions are humble because they set their sights on serving the Savior—the highest goal imaginable. As Charles Spurgeon puts it, "This is Heaven to a saint: in all things to serve the Lord Christ, and to be owned by Him as His servant is our soul's high ambition for eternity."[13]

7

Ambition's Contentment

IF AMBITION DEFINES ME,
IT WILL NEVER FULFILL ME

If church history were a dojo, the English Puritans would all be black belts. Seriously, they had some staggering insights into the Christian life. But when you read them, you have to wonder: did these guys get paid by the word? Long words, long sentences, long paragraphs, long books. Even the abridgments of their books are long.

But in combing through all that Puritan writing, you'll inevitably stumble on a statement that's crisp, clear, and short enough to make you think for a long time: "If we have not what we desire, we have more than we deserve."[1]

In this brief sentence from his classic book *The Art of Divine Contentment*, Thomas Watson sketches the portrait of a saint at peace. On its face, contentment seems at odds with ambition, doesn't it? But for us to be rescued from selfish ambition, the warm colors of godly contentment must be mixed with the bright colors of godly ambition. Let's see why this is important and what it creates.

The Problem: We Have Not What We Desire

The sunny day hardly matched Walt's mood. Even though it had happened six months ago, Walt still couldn't believe Monique was given the job he deserved.

Sure, Monique was qualified, but Walt had always dreamed of occupying that position. He'd prayed for it over the last two years, patiently biding his time until the position opened. Walt was a competitor. He played fair but hard, and he wasn't used to losing. But he'd lost out. And though he would never say it out loud, it galled him that he lost to a woman. This felt like total failure.

Now Walt felt as if his star was no longer rising in the company. For the first time in his life, he felt like "all the others." He just knew his boss no longer saw him as a go-to guy—he could feel it in his voice. "He's lost confidence in me," Walt would whisper to himself during his hourly self-counseling sessions. "He says I'm still vital to the department, but it just doesn't feel that way." He couldn't shake the feeling that he was shrinking right before everybody's eyes.

His wife suggested he was looking at this all wrong. She reminded him of his good health, his loving family, his stock options, and even his Christianity. Then she forced the issue on his not getting the promotion: "Why does this bother you so much?"

It was a great question, but Walt couldn't come up with an answer.

His confusion led to new feelings of disorientation, as if he were lost or set adrift at sea. Walt increasingly felt the glow of his life dimming, like a smoldering wick in desperate search of a spark.

To use Watson's words, Walt would have to admit, "I have not what I desire." He held ambitions for the promotion, worked for it, prayed for it, but didn't get it. And God wasn't phoning in to offer any explanations.

Was God out to lunch when Monique got promoted? Was he momentarily diverted by some surprise in the Middle East? Nope. God willed Monique's ascent, even though Walt wanted it.

When God acts contrary to our will, disappointment is understandable.

When God acts contrary to our will, disappointment is understandable. But when our desires go unfulfilled and disappointment begins to define us, something else is afoot. It's called discontentment.

Discontentment rears its head when our ambitions are frustrated. We aspire to something that seems perfectly legit, but God seems to bail on his part of the bargain. So we stew in self-pity and wonder why God is so sloppy in the way he does business. Discontentment is a herald announcing that there was more to our ambitions than noble aspirations. And God loves us too much to keep us in the dark.

Walt's ambitions became engorged with self. Sure, he wanted the role to use the gifts and talents God had given him. That was real and valuable. But a more dangerous agenda took control. Walt began to invest the promotion with identity. As he faced daily the routine of his job, he began to want more . . . to *need* more. He decided he had to be seen as a player; he needed folks to think he could run with the big dogs. His heart jumped from desire to demand.

But God loved Walt too much to answer that prayer. Closing the door on that ambition was actually God's protection. Sometimes God's care means he doesn't fulfill our desires.

To want more responsibility isn't wrong. It can be a healthy sign of godly ambition. But sometimes our real motive is revealed when our ambition is rejected. The job went to Monique, and Walt tanked. The evil wasn't his ambition; it was ambition swollen with self.

Walt lost the job, but his discontentment got a huge promotion. When selfish ambitions are unsatisfied, we grow discontent.

The Solution: We Have More than We Deserve

When we don't have what we desire, it's important to acknowledge that. We would be foolish to ignore it. If what we lack becomes our primary focus, ambition becomes contaminated with self.

If you want an ambition that screens out self and shrinks discontentment, mull over this idea: we already possess far more than we deserve. If that statement intrigues you, keep reading. There's more to come.

How can Walt be helped? How should we respond when blocked ambitions open the door to discontentment? Where do we go when we're haunted and taunted with "By now, I should have been . . ."? What do we do when we don't have what we desire?

What does it even look like to realize we have more than we deserve?

To answer these questions, we must again visit another man familiar with ambition.

Contentment Requires a Proper Perspective

Suppose you read the following as a quote from a famous spiritual adviser:

Not that I am speaking of being in need, for I have learned in whatever situation I am to be content. I know how to be brought low, and I know how to abound. In any and every circumstance, I have learned the secret of facing plenty and hunger, abundance and need. I can do all things through him who strengthens me.

What would be your mental picture of the author of those words? Some mystic hermit on a mountaintop? A former business tycoon who sold it all for life on a sailboat? Oprah Winfrey?

Believe it or not, it came from a prisoner—from Paul, as recorded in Philippians 4:11–13.

Paul, the man of action, was shut down in prison (Philippians 1:13). Death was on his mind (1:20–23). On top of that, his dear friends in the Philippian church were experiencing attacks from outside (1:15–17, 28–30) and divisions from within (2:2–4; 4:2–3). Paul isn't offering the calm reflections of a philosopher deep in contemplation. He's desperate to protect the church, preach and preserve the truth, and troubleshoot the burgeoning problems—those were his ambitions. They seem pretty noble, don't they? Certainly God would throw open Paul's jail cell for that.

But Paul couldn't follow through on them. The God who had sent him out had now confined him to a prison. No phone, no Internet, no videoconferencing, no networking with other leaders in the field. The only ways to act on his ambitions were inefficient and vicarious—writing letters or sending envoys. If that was my scenario, discontentment would already be a done deal. But Paul learned a different response. He did not have what he desired, but he knew he had something better.

"Not that I am speaking of being in need," he writes, "for I have learned in whatever situation I am to be content."

Hold on. Paul was in prison, but not in need. He wanted that to be clear. In chapter 4 he's grateful for their financial support but doesn't "need" it. Not because he's flush with cash, but because he's learned something in life. He possesses what Jeremiah Burroughs called "the rare jewel of Christian contentment."

Good for Paul, you say. But what does that mean? Paul had happy thoughts and a big dopey grin?

Contentment means *being satisfied and at peace with God's will in all situations*. It's a state of the soul where your desires conform to wherever you find yourself.

In Philippians we discover something that marks the life of every believer. On the one hand, we're called to "strain forward to what lies ahead" and "press on toward the goal for the prize of the upward call of God in Christ Jesus" (3:13–14). But we're also given Paul's example of learning "in whatever situation I am to be content" (4:11). Is Paul confused? He seems to be saying, "Hunger for more" in one chapter, and "Be happy with where you are" in the next.

Exactly.

Since Paul's ambitions were not selfish,
he could live with them unfulfilled.

Since Paul's ambitions were not selfish, he could live with them unfulfilled. Sure, he had dreams and desires—but they were God-focused, not Paul-focused. If they remained unsatisfied, that was God's business. So Paul was able to aspire for more while resting peacefully in what God provided. He hungered for more but was happy with less. Deferred dreams didn't eat away at him. Paul could be at peace in the present without abandoning hopes for the future.

Selfish ambition is a motivating desire to do things for selfish glory. Godly ambition is a motivating desire to do things for God's glory. Contentment is what happens when godly ambition triumphs over selfish ambition. Where there is godly ambition, we can be at peace with whatever comes our way.

Paul's Lesson

Being hungry for more but content with less—this is no skate. Charles Spurgeon said, "This surely is the highest degree in *humanities* to which a man can possibly attain, to have learned in whatsoever state he is, to be content."[2] Mr. Spurgeon was talking about advanced degrees; if you're like me, you're still finger-painting in the kindergarten class of the school of contentment. But that's not where we're supposed to stay.

Sometimes when God delays our ambitions, we try to—and I know this is crazy—*punish* him by pulling our dreams off the table. "God, you didn't deliver, so I'm not entrusting my hopes and dreams to you. So there!" Yes, it's crazy. But if you can relate to that, or if you feel like you just don't have the whole contentment thing nailed down, Paul has some encouraging words.

"I have *learned* . . ."

I have to admit I wish it came differently. Wouldn't it be great to have contentment in pill form or as something you could grab at the self-checkout? Not in this life. It must be learned. "I have learned in whatever situation I am to be content."

I once read this about Jonathan Edwards: "He appeared like a Man of God, whose happiness was out of the reach of his enemies."[3] I think that means Edwards learned contentment. His peace wasn't dependent upon how he was treated by others. Even when others sinned against him, he was peaceful and satisfied with God's will. We know Jonathan Edwards was ambitious. This was a guy who was writing theological treatises at the age of seventeen. But it's encouraging to know that he had also "learned to be content."

Learning to live contentedly when we don't have what we desire is one powerful antidote to selfish ambitions. But walking in the tension between godly ambition for the future and contentment in the present is no easy thing.

No wonder Paul says he'd learned the "secret" of facing both plenty and hunger. This isn't the kind of secret we can open a fortune cookie and discover. Contentment is something acquired when faith is applied over time in those we-have-not-what-we-desire seasons of life.

Nobody likes the school of contentment. But everybody who wants to glorify God will get an education there.

Paul's Constraints

Paul specifies the field of play for contentment. Bracketing the field are two end zones—two life experiences where contentment engages ambitions. "I know how to be brought low, and I know how to abound. In any and every circumstance, I have learned the secret of facing plenty and hunger, abundance and need."

All of life is played out somewhere on this field. In one end zone are the times when ambitions are satisfied. Paul uses words like "abound," "plenty," "abundance." He's talking about the good times: you get a raise, you get pregnant, you land the account, you nail the "A," you're engaged! Dreams are coming alive, and life is getting good.

Down at the other end of the field lies the opposite zone, where ambitions are starved. Paul describes this as being "brought low," "facing hunger," "need." The hard times.

At both ends of the field, Paul says, he has learned the secret of contentment.

THE TEST OF PROSPERITY

In times of plenty, ambitions are often fat, happy, and ready to party. Yet Paul says, "*I know how* to abound." Is that really something you have to learn? My first instinct is to think, *Go ahead, Lord, test me with prosperity. Just gimme a Lexus—I can take it!* Yeah, I can do abounding. But I don't think that's what Paul had in mind. Abounding wisely and biblically is much harder than it appears.

Paul needed to learn how to abound because with great blessing comes unexpected temptation. "The Christian far oftener disgraces his profession in prosperity than when he is being abased," Spurgeon said.[4] Having your ambitions satisfied can be a double-edged sword for the follower of Christ.

"The crucible is for silver, and the furnace is for gold, and a man is tested by his praise" (Prov. 27:21). That's from Solomon, the wisest man in history. Think about what he's saying. For precious metals, a crucible and furnace both play the same role—they test by heat. But Solomon is detecting a danger that's largely overlooked in cultures like ours where affirmation is viewed as an inalienable right. Praise has a way of enflaming desires, and that tends to surface the heart's impurities.

But don't think of "praise" here as simply people encouraging you. "Great job, Johnny!" It's more than that, because praise comes in many forms. Bonuses at work are praise; so are promotions.

Birthday parties, sorority initiations, frequent flyer miles, winning Best Lawn in the Neighborhood. When you think about it, we have no lack of voices telling us we're great in some way, for some reason.

When we hear "test," we think of things we want to avoid, like poverty and persecution. But you're more likely to find yourself in another kind of test. It comes in times of abounding, abundance, and plenty. Solomon calls it the test of praise.

When praise comes our way, does it make us more humble or hungry for more praise?

Where does our heart go when praise comes our way? Does it make us more humble or hungry for more praise?

When praise meets godly ambitions, it inspires gratitude toward God. One telltale sign of godliness in our ambitions is how easily we transfer honor to God, recognizing him as the source and power of our performance. Why? Because we did it for his glory in the first place.

But when we crave our own glory, we keep praise to ourselves. We don't pass it along. Like a gluttonous prince, we feast on every morsel, then demand a larger portion.

In the book of Esther, the adviser Haman was promoted to top dog under the king. Everyone bowed to pay homage to him—except a Jewish man named Mordecai. Haman went rabid and announced he would exterminate all the Jews. God intervened, Mordecai was protected, and Haman found infamy at the end of a noose. Such was his hunt for honor: Haman was ready to exterminate an entire ethnic group because one man wouldn't praise him. His heart was certainly revealed.

If we're sinfully ambitious, praise from others ironically stirs discontent. An ambitious lay leader with a strong dose of selfishness will misconstrue praise as a calling to consolidate his power base in the church. An employee with a self-seeking desire for upward mobility will reinterpret unsolicited honor as a call to jockey for her boss's job.

Praise is the prophet that reveals the heart. Maybe that's what

Bono means when he says, "It's no secret [that] ambition bites the nail of success."[5] Now that I've offered the obligatory Bono quote, I'll admit that I like Solomon's twist better: a man is tested by his praise.

THE TEST OF ADVERSITY

Although we'd like to live permanently in the "abounding" end of the field, we're sometimes pushed to the other end, where dreams go to die. You're passed over at work, you flunk the class, your business goes broke, a friend disappoints, the leader you respect fails, retirement is forced, the pregnancy test is negative again. Your dreams are on a respirator gasping for air. In times like these, ambitions mock you without pity. You have not what you desire.

Did you ever wish you could edit out some parts of your life? I want it to be like reality TV—we keep the exciting clips and edit out the rest. But real life isn't reality TV. (Actually, there's little reality in reality TV.) Real life isn't made up of isolated and edited clips from the day. Reality is not an endless parade of progress. It's about fits and starts and interruptions, never convenient, always disruptive.

One day I was sitting in our family room with my wife, reading. At one point she heard water running in the basement and asked who was in the basement shower. I said I didn't know and went back to reading.

Moments later, a stray thought pierced my consciousness, yanking me out of book-land and back into the real world of home ownership: *Wait a minute; we don't have a basement shower!*

Running downstairs, I immediately detected that all was not right. I was able to discern this because water was shooting out of my wall like someone had tripped a fire hydrant. It was pretty awesome, actually. I was tempted to just stand there and watch, but then I remembered it was my house.

For some reason, I'd missed the what-to-do-when-pipes-break-and-you-need-to-shut-down-the-water-really-quickly class in high school. It must have been on one of the days I was skipping to indulge in, uh, extracurriculars. The best I could muster in that moment was to run around the house looking for a light switch to throw while screaming, "A pipe has burst, a pipe has burst!"

I'm really glad my dad wasn't there.

Eventually my neighbor heard the commotion and walked in and shut down the water. Andrew is one of those handy guys who knows how to do everything and can shut off water simply by waving his hand like Yoda. He waved his hand, the water shut off, and I was left standing in my three-inch basement sea wondering when the tide would go out.

Real life rarely knocks. It just breaks down the door itching for someone to level.

Real life rarely knocks. It just breaks down the door itching for someone to level.

When Paul found contentment even as life broke down his doors, he learned to be brought low with a low I can't comprehend. His contentment wasn't based on where he was or what he was doing. Whether he was preaching before King Agrippa or penning letters in prison, he was equally satisfied in God. Paul's contentment wasn't situational—based on where he was or what he was doing. He could enjoy God the same way in plenty or want.

What do we do when dreams and life don't intersect? When life seems to force us down rather than lift us up?

Charles Simeon, the pastor who persevered in preaching when people boycotted his services and locked the pews, faced a different crisis at another point in his life when his health broke down. He spent eight months recuperating while a younger man named Thomas Thomason stepped in to preach in Trinity Church.

Reverend Thomason became quite the preacher, a more-than-able replacement. It led Charles Simeon to quote John the Baptist: "He must increase, but I must decrease" (John 3:30). Simeon then told a friend, "Now I see why I have been laid aside. I bless God for it."[6] In a world that understands only ascent and upward mobility, that's a stunning statement.

"I must decrease" may have been sufficient for John the Baptist or Charles Simeon, but for us it's considered a curse, a sign our dreams are being put out to pasture. Simeon later rallied and was able to go back to his pulpit. But it doesn't always work that way. For those times we need to learn to be "brought low."

Have you learned to look at the times you've been laid aside and say, "I bless God for it"? Packer writes, "The world's idea that everyone, from childhood up, should be able at all times to succeed in measurable ways, and that it is a great disgrace not to, hangs over the Christian community like a pall of acrid smoke."[7] God help us to smell the smoke so we don't fail the test.

Contentment Requires Divine Power

To complete the lesson, Paul wants us to understand the source of his ability to be content: "I can do all things through him who strengthens me" (Phil. 4:13).

The strengthener he mentions is Jesus Christ. Paul is returning us to the source of his strength and the cause of his contentment. Sinclair Ferguson tells us that the words "through him" might be better translated as "in him."[8] The strength to do all things and be satisfied at all times comes from the Savior. Contentment is learned in Christ. That means we become experts at examining and enjoying what it truly means to be in him—the abundance that comes to us because of what Christ has done for us. This is *our* source of strength, helping us enjoy contentment while the world strives. It also circles us back to Thomas Watson's words: "If we have not what we desire, we have more than we deserve."

At the heart of discontent lies this conviction: "I don't have what I deserve." The gospel answers with this cheery news: "You're absolutely right. And you can thank God for that!" The gospel turns our complaint on its head and reminds us that regardless of our state— high or low, plenty or hunger, abundance or need—we live infinitely above what we really deserve.

Let me spin a parable to drive this home.

A man once lived a modest life. His house was small, his income scanty, his food meager. He often complained, "Lord, I've served you faithfully, given regularly, and sought to honor you in all I do. Why haven't I prospered? I deserve more!"

One night he had a dream. He was walking along a river. As he came close to a bridge, he saw a homeless man sitting on a cardboard box. The man's hair was matted, his clothes tattered. He sat slurping cold soup from a rusty can.

Seeing someone near, the homeless man said, "Lord, what must it be like to be wealthy, like this man approaching?"

The first man heard the prayer, and he stopped in his tracks. He was smitten like George Bailey and went away yelling out to any who would listen, "It's a wonderful life!" *After all,* he thought, *I'm way better off than that dude.*

Now here's the thing: many people think that's the heart of contentment—*just realize how good you have it! Life could be so much worse.* The key to contentment, in other words, is just to compare ourselves with those in less favorable conditions. Roll the poverty pictures and cue the gratitude, contentment is coming to town.

Godly contentment has to be more than being thankful you're better off than someone else.

But we never find true, lasting contentment by comparing ourselves with others. Godly contentment has to be more than being thankful you're better off than someone else. If our joy is ultimately founded on the it-could-be-worse model, then our contentment is, at best, situational. And Paul's words of exhortation will bounce off our obstinate hearts. After all, the feelings will eventually fade, and the contrast will be lost.

True contentment comes by comparing what we have *to what our sins deserve.* That means we find it in the gospel.

> The more absorbed I am in the gospel, the more grateful I become in the midst of my circumstances, whatever they may be. . . . When I look at any circumstance that God apportions me, I am *first* grateful for the wrath I am *not* receiving in that moment. . . . Secondly, I am grateful for the blessings that are given to me instead of His wrath. This two-layered gratitude disposes my heart to give thanks in all things and it also lends a certain intensity to my giving of thanks.[9]

The gospel escorts us beyond the bridge of comparison with others. In the gospel we're reminded that we were spiritually wretched, lost, miserable, and broken—destitute before God. Even worse, we stood powerless to alter our circumstances. Worse still, we didn't even *want* to alter our circumstances. We were hostile toward help. Our life was hopeless, and our end was torment in eternal flames. And we were content to be left alone.

But in his boundless mercy, God came to us in the person of Christ. He reached out to us and wrenched us free from our irrational commitment to our own destruction. By dying in our place, he gave us reason and hope to live again. We became spiritually rich beyond our wildest imagination as we were adopted into the family of God. We who deserved perpetual punishment received an eternal inheritance.

We were worthy of nothing more than hell.

We got heaven.

Do you have all you desire? Me neither. But we have more than we deserve.

The Depth of Contentment

Included in the eternal inheritance that was granted us in Christ is personal access to an always good, always loving, always wise heavenly Father. The circumstances in our lives are handcrafted by God for our good and for his glory. The man of modest means and the man under the bridge can both rest contented, knowing their lot in life is God's will, God's plan, and ultimately God's doing.

> I have what I have from the love of God, and have it sanctified to me by God, and I have it free of cost from God by the purchase of the blood of Jesus Christ, and I have it as a forerunner of those eternal mercies that are reserved for me, and in this my soul rejoices.[10]

Remember Walt, who was discontented after missing out on the promotion he craved? God orchestrated Walt's career without that promotion, while he also planned Monique's career to include it. It was also God's doing that Charles Simeon was replaced and surpassed in the pulpit by his friend.

The abounding ambitions that have been realized in your life are God's doing—and so are the ambitions that have been laid low. All are God's doing. We have all we have, and what we have, because we have God.

So, if you don't have what you desire, take heart, take comfort, and heed this: you have more than you deserve.

Contentment Requires Daily Practice

Remember when Paul said, "I have *learned* . . . to be content"? We aren't hardwired with contentment. So if we're to find the place of rest Paul found, we have to work toward it, and be ambitious for it. It requires some real doing on our part. We must practice contentment on a daily basis.

To help you, here are a couple of approaches that have been enormously helpful in my own journey of learning contentment.

MEDITATE ON THINGS ABOVE

In his instructions to Christians, Paul regularly reminds us to set our minds on "things that are above" (Col. 3:1–2) and to renew our minds (Rom. 12:2). That's because the battle for satisfaction in the present and ambition for the future is fought on the turf of our mind.

The gospel is the highest truth we can ponder. So think about it—often! It reminds us of how God's love was most vividly expressed by sending his Son, who "laid down his life for us" (1 John 3:16). Pondering God's love redirects our minds from what we think we lack to the undeserved gift we've been given.

My "beautiful mind" can get pretty overactive. I can spin out a prophecy of doom from almost any tidbit of information. Maybe your mind is like that. Maybe for you a headache isn't a mere headache but the symptom of a massive brain tumor. A knock under the hood is automatically the transmission giving up the ghost. A grunt from your teenager is sufficient evidence he's joined a gang.

You know what I'm talking about. We ponder our misery better than our mercies.

Unless we corral those thoughts, they'll distract our ambitions and swipe our joy. Think of something better. Think often of God's love. The fact that you and I aren't presently in hell is an expression of God's love. You don't have what you desire? You *do* have God's love.

If your own beautiful mind is taking you to ugly places, here are some ways to bring it back to the corral of gospel truth.

You don't have what you desire?
You do have God's love.

Take up the practice of Scripture memorization. Not just isolated memory verses, but God's truth in context. Chapters like Philippians 4 or Ephesians 1 or Matthew 6 or Psalm 16. Memorizing sections of Scripture is mental work that forces us to ponder biblical arguments, not disconnected truths.

Another thing I do is discipline myself to seize opportunities to thank God privately and publicly for the daily, easily overlooked blessings in my life. Like the fact that I wake up each morning and there's no smelly dog next to my bed. The fact that I have a car I can drive to where I want to go. The fact that the traffic lights sometimes stay green when I'm in a hurry to get there. All these are occasions for genuine thankfulness.

You'll be surprised at how much this kind of habit of gratitude will open your eyes to see God's goodness all around you.

MOVE HIGH BY REACHING LOW

A second practice plan is to move high by reaching low.

I love how Jesus drops into the real world to make eternal points. While talking to the disciples about their addiction to honor, he brought up seating arrangements at wedding feasts. His words were as sage as they were streetwise. Don't take the best seat, he said, lest you get bumped by someone more important and find yourself becoming part of the evening's entertainment. Instead sit in the lowest seat because the host may prefer to elevate you. Then he adds, "For everyone who exalts himself will be humbled, and he who humbles himself will be exalted" (Luke 14:11).

Remember, Jesus isn't against ambition. He encourages the pursuit of greatness. God has clear ideas about the career path for greatness. It *descends*—unlike the world's way.

The world fears descending. It flees from any situation where descending is a possibility. But we're to actually choose that path for ourselves. It's not a new idea. It originated with Jesus. So seek him, and we'll find our place. "Have your hearts filled with Christ," says Charles Hodge. "The more we know of him, the more we appreciate his excellence and claims, the less shall we desire to be great in ourselves."[11]

> Contentment comes as we satisfy the
> fierce ambition to move higher by reaching lower.

Contentment comes as we satisfy the fierce ambition to move higher by reaching lower. We're filled as we choose to empty.

Two of the best ways I've found of reaching lower is to regularly confess my sins and weaknesses and to regularly invite the input of others into my life. I wonder what would have happened to the guy in Jesus' parable if he'd been aware that he didn't belong at the head of the table in the first place. Having a sober assessment of our strengths and weaknesses from honest and knowledgeable friends will keep us grounded in reality. And confessing our sins and temptations, particularly when it comes to pride and ambition, will keep us focused more on our need for grace than on our next upward promotion.

Set Your Sights beyond Contentment

Neither you nor I have all we desire. But together we've learned something. We have more than we deserve. Way more. If we can get fired up to do exploits for God and peacefully rest in the results, whatever they may be, we'll move closer to him.

I guarantee we won't get all we desire. But we'll get way more than we deserve.

There's an old saying: "Graveyards are filled with indispensable people." It's a great reminder of an eternal truth. We're all decaying. That means we're all in decline; whether you're in the spring, summer, fall, or winter of life, you're going to be replaced. Whatever position you hold right now that fires your passion is only yours for a season.

The only irreplaceable position is the one occupied by the Savior who's seated next to the Father interceding for us.

Does the thought of your own decline depress you? It's supposed to be a liberating thought. Our ambitions, and therefore our contentment, are so often tied to the circumstantial mountains and valleys of life, but whatever we obtain here is never ours forever. We'll have to give it up—if at no other time, then when we leave this mortal coil.

The key is to not tie our contentment to changeable things. For it to rest secure, contentment must be anchored into something that's never replaced. Perhaps Sinclair Ferguson sums it up best:

> Christian contentment . . . is the direct fruit of having no higher ambition than to belong to the Lord and to be totally at His disposal in the place He appoints, at the time He chooses, with the provision He is pleased to make.[12]

What more could we truly desire?

8

Ambitious Failure

WHERE IS GOD WHEN OUR DREAMS LEAD TO DEFEATS?

Coming down from the pulpit is always an adventure. Preaching God's Word can lift a man to heaven; answering questions afterwards usually drops him back to earth.

One Sunday, out of the corner of my eye, I saw Jake. I knew immediately the message had stirred his stew. He stood there waiting—patient, earnest, intense. We shook hands, and he dropped his question on me.

"What do I do when my ambitions set me up to fail?"

Jake isn't his actual name, but his story's quite real. Jake graduated from college with a Dickensian sense of great expectations. He was bright, gifted, and armed with aspirations. First, he wanted to be a highly skilled software developer. That's reasonable enough. Good job, Jake. But check out these next two.

As an engineer, he wanted to fundamentally change the face of software development—to do for software what Bill Gates did for Microsoft, what Steve Jobs did for Apple, or what George Lucas did for light sabers.

And with the stellar financial profits from that endeavor, Jake ultimately wanted to serve as a pastor-teacher in a local church . . . for free.

So off he went into the land of software development to make his dreams come true. Just two years into his moderately successful job, his ship arrived. An offer for the perfect position, coupled with grand promises of responsibility and leadership, put him on the fast track of dream fulfillment. To top it off, his church asked him to lead a portion of ministry, the beginning of the final piece of his goal-setting trifecta.

However, not all dreams in Softwaresville come true. Circumstances changed, and the job became a source of stress, even dread. The recruiter who made all those promises was replaced by someone less than convinced of Jake's ability. The new guy basically gave him the boot.

Jake was laid low, with all his torn and tattered goals in hand. A few years earlier, his success had been just a matter of time; he was zealous, confident to the brim. Now he was jobless, goalless, and hopeless. A self-described failure.

Introducing Failure

Failure. It's an equal opportunity affliction visiting rich and poor alike. Failure defies and levels and confounds even the best laid plans.

Failure is as old as history itself. Just flip through your Bible. Adam and Eve add the wrong fruit to their diet. Babel breaks ground on a skyscraper that fails the ultimate inspection. Abram sells out his wife to save his skin. Samson rejects the good girls and weds Delilah. God's people demand and get a worldly king, who then tries to kill his replacement. David—the replacement—lusts for Bathsheba. Peter says, "Jesus who?" Paul and Barnabas split.

Like death, taxes, and really bad haircuts, failure finds us all.

I hear you: "What grand news, Dave! As long as we're discussing my inevitable failure, why not just tell me I'm overweight and odoriferous?"

First, I'm not totally sure what *odoriferous* means, so I would never call you that.

Second, if God is truly sovereign, there must be a place for our failure in his plan. From Genesis to Revelation, the Bible declares God's supreme control over events. If he can't work through our screwups, he's guilty of false advertising.

Like it or not, the sovereign God is Lord over our failures. In fact, he works through them. Failure isn't simply God's nightstick to whack us into submission. It's an experience where we can discover God's love, his irresistible grace, and the true potency of the gospel.

But to get to those discoveries, we must see failure as the place where some ambitions go to die so other things might come alive.

A Diagnosis of Failure

The clouds of potential failure can often ground ambition before it even gets off the launching pad.

Most people view failure like the flu—avoid it at all costs. We stay away from others who fail, as if we're afraid we might be infected with failure germs. That's a bit shortsighted, not to mention insufficiently biblical.

Don't get me wrong. I'm not trying to pioneer a new paradigm that makes failure a goal worth pursuing. (Johnny wants to go bankrupt; "Go, Johnny, go!") And I'm certainly not suggesting we overlook our foolish choices that lead to failure. We must always distinguish between the act of failing—which often relates to our sin, weakness, or limitations—and God's purposes in allowing us to fail.

But since studies prove that 100 percent of human beings fail at some point, it may be time to understand it better.

Failure typically comes from a couple of sources. First, we fail because we're not God. While God is self-sufficient, we're dependent. God knows all; we know little. God is wise; we can be foolish. God is all-powerful; we're weak. So sometimes we fail just because we're human and unable to exercise perfect judgment or anticipate all contingencies. We make simple (sometimes stupid) mistakes—a poor investment, or relying too much on Web site information, or thinking we can carry two paint cans up the ladder at the same time. Nobody's intentionally sinning here, but there's a big "oops" at the end of the process. These are the little failures of life, the pebble-in-the-shoe variety that dents the skin but doesn't stop the walk.

There's also a darker reason for failure, and we can't avoid talking about it. Sometimes we fail because of sin—we speak callously, respond angrily, covet secretly, nurture jealousy, lust uncontrollably. We fail at fulfilling God's Word.

It happened again the other day. I spoke harshly to my youngest daughter. I didn't love her with my words or guide her with my example. I didn't display the gospel through my actions. Dress it up any way you want, but the reality remains: I sinned. I failed. I thank God for grace that convicted me and prompted my repentance. It was a fresh reminder that not all failure is sin, but all sin is failure.

Maybe the worst type of failure is the unannounced, smash-mouth, big and hairy, knock-you-to-the-ground failure, the kind that leaves you dazed and wondering who you really are. Jake experienced some of that, but there are other more prominent examples. Think of the star athlete with a driving ambition to be more than good—he wants to be the greatest. So a little juice here, a little cream there, and his performance-enhanced stats put him at the top of his game. Until a random test turns his legend into a myth, and nobody wants his autograph anymore. His dreams collapse into dust.

Where is God when our highest ambition leads to our greatest defeat?

Large ambitions open the door to bigger disasters.

With ambition comes failure. Small ambitions can lead to small failures, like the new recipe that results in a culinary disaster. Large ambitions open the door to bigger disasters. The famous eighteenth-century explorer James Cook once said, "I . . . had ambition not only to go farther than any man had ever been before, but as far as it was possible for a man to go."[1] Cook's last voyage ended when he was savagely slain by Polynesian islanders. His ambition took him as far as he could go, and it cost him his life.

Maybe how to handle failure isn't a theoretical question for you. Your failure visits you almost every day, bearing miserable tidings from the past. You're left constantly wondering what you should do. Talk about it yet again? Break out the sackcloth? Schedule an appearance on *Dr. Phil*?

The biblical message is not merely that we should handle failure well. It's that God works miraculously in failure for his glory and our godliness. The divine perspective on human failure is this: *failure is ambition refused for a better plan.*

Does that seem hard to swallow?

If so, you're not alone. But let's look how it was displayed in the story of a remarkable young man.

Failure as Ambition Refused

One of the most significant events in the spread of the gospel throughout the world over the past three centuries occurred in 1749 with the publishing of *The Life of David Brainerd*. This small book had a curious beginning.

The great preacher Jonathan Edwards had befriended a sickly young man and brought him into his home to recuperate. The young man, David Brainerd, acquired a serious illness in a lonely and arduous ministry to the American Indians on the colonial frontier. He would never recover. He passed away at the age of twenty-nine in Edwards's home, leaving behind all his earthly possessions. Among them were personal diaries that Edwards began to read in earnest. Believing the diaries contained rich spiritual insight from a man of uncommon godliness, Edwards edited and published the material as *The Life of David Brainerd*. Little did Edwards know this small volume was to become the most widely read, reprinted, and influential of all his works for more than a century. Countless missionaries, including Henry Martyn, William Carey, Robert Murray McCheyne, and Jim Elliot, were inspired to the mission field by Brainerd's story.[2]

And yet, were it not for the single most devastating failure of Brainerd's life, his missionary efforts would have never gotten off the ground.

Brainerd was born in 1718 in a small Connecticut town. Raised by devout Puritan parents until he was orphaned at fourteen, he was swept up in the Great Awakening and powerfully converted at the age of twenty-one. Fueled by ambition for pastoral ministry, he enrolled in Yale College to receive the necessary training.

As a third-year student, Brainerd had proven himself to be bright, articulate, and at the top of his class. But like all of us, his tongue wasn't as smart as his brain. The overthrow of his dream came through a tongue too often loosed with immature fervor. According to Edwards's biography of him, young Brainerd's character was colored by an "intemperate, indiscreet zeal."[3] That's Edwards's way of saying that Brainerd had a big mouth and knew how to use it.

In an ill-timed display of that youthful indiscretion, Brainerd criticized one of his tutors, Chauncey Whittelsey, announcing that he "has no more grace than a chair," and wondered that the man "did not drop down dead" for his lack of support toward students awakened by God.[4] But Yale wasn't looking for customer feedback. Though he'd nearly completed the work for his degree and was about to graduate at the head of his class,[5] Brainerd was immediately expelled.

To complicate things, one needed a university degree to pastor in Connecticut. This meant that Brainerd's remark was a career-ending comment. It shut the door to church ministry, cutting off oxygen to his ultimate dream.

Shortly after the incident, he confessed, "I seem to be declining, with respect to my life and warmth in divine things; have not had so free access to God in prayer to-day as usual of late."[6] Brainerd didn't see it yet, but God was refusing his ambition for a better plan.

The Better Plan for Being Laid Low

As failure works its humbling grace, the better plan activates. Do we see it unfold? It's those stomach-turning moments we all hate. Our rapid ascent stalls, we fall to earth with a thud, and we stumble blindly about trying to pick up the pieces of our broken plans.

Think about the situations experienced by people you know: the airtight business plan that went belly-up; the dream house that never factored in the unexpected layoff; the engagement ring and bended knee that encountered an unexpected "No, I can't marry you"; the construction costs that came in at double the estimate; the marriage that unexpectedly dissolved; the evangelistic strategy that bore little fruit. You know, the stuff of life.

These aren't heady moments when we're tempted to exalt in our intellect or talent. They're a shock to the system. They throw a fist to the jaw of our desires. They become defining moments as God commands our attention to rescue our ambitions from their earthbound aspirations.

Failure humanizes us. It reconnects us with the reality that there's a vast difference between having an ambition and satisfying it.

For our ambitions to go well, we're dependent upon God. Only he is omnicompetent and able to achieve all he desires. Only he can satisfy his ambitions at all times. The rest of us have a pretty pathetic batting average. And that's by merciful design, because it disabuses us of the illusion that we're in charge of our lives.

Failure reconnects us with the vast difference between having an ambition and satisfying it.

It's God's way of removing our glory and restoring his own. God will lay low anyone who competes for his supremacy. Our dreams crumble, and in desperation we reach out to God and his rock-solid promises. In the cleft of his Word, our vision of God grows, and we shrink to our rightful place.

In humbly responding to God's purpose in our failure, the first step is to acknowledge it. I'm sure that David Brainerd was tempted to rationalize his situation and maybe even blame others for it; I mean, he was human, right? Still, those closest to him remarked that he never focused on the punishment he received at Yale. Instead he owned the wrong he'd committed. This work of contrition resulted in a sincere and heartfelt confession to everyone he offended—beginning with the holy God to whom he owed primary allegiance.

> I humbly confess, that herein I have sinned against God, and acted contrary to the rules of his word, and have injured Mr. Whittelsey. I had no right to make thus free with his character; and had no just reason to say as I did concerning him. My fault herein was the more aggravated, in that I said this concerning one that was so much my superior, and one that I was obliged to treat with special respect and honour, by reason of the relation I stood in to him in the college. . . . I have often reflected on this act with grief; I hope, on account of the sin of it: and am willing to lie low, and be abased before God and man for it. And humbly ask the forgiveness of the governors of the college, and of the whole society; but of Mr. Whittelsey in particular.[7]

And Edwards writes,

> I was a witness to the very Christian spirit which Brainerd showed at that time. . . . There truly appeared in him a great degree of

calmness and humility; without the least appearance of rising of spirit for any ill-treatment which he supposed he had suffered, or the least backwardness to abase himself before those, who, as he thought, had wronged him. What he did was without any objection or appearance of reluctance, even in private to his friends, to whom he freely opened himself.[8]

I know what you're thinking: *Now comes the payoff.* The humbled hero has learned his lesson, and in a Hollywood-style, last-minute reversal Yale reinstates him. Right?

Not even close. The administration remained unmoved. Under no circumstances was Brainerd permitted to finish his degree. His dream to pastor had to die.

Sometimes providence allows a punishment beyond what the failure requires. God is just, but he's able to use apparent injustice for his purpose in our lives. Maybe you've met the guy who gets seriously nailed the first time he cuts a corner (the same corner others have safely cut for years). Or the parent who erupts once at an umpire and is forever labeled as the Little League big mouth. Maybe for years Brainerd was known as "Almost a Yalie." Life's like that sometimes. Our lowest moments become our biggest label. But David Brainerd was willing "to lie low, and be abased before God and man for it."[9] It was his failure; he was willing to accept the full consequences.

Though he was denied his dream because of his failure, something more important than ministry fulfillment was at stake. Whatever pride David Brainerd had in his gifts or accomplishment took a mortal blow in this experience. God attacked something that needed to go so Brainerd could become something he was called to be.

Meanwhile, God became bigger and more precious to him.

Giving up his ambition kindled something else in his heart. As Brainerd humbled himself before God, clarity came for his next assignment. In God's plan, Brainerd's hard-won humility would allow him to become God's spokesman for people who had never heard his name before.

As a pastor for more than two decades, I've noticed a curious thing. There are certain kinds of entrenched pride that only failure uproots. Scripture says it this way: "Let anyone who thinks that he stands take heed lest he fall" (1 Cor. 10:12). God has a special training program for those who think they stand, for the men and women who think, *My success is locked down, my reputation unimpeachable, and my future under control—all because of me!* It's to these God says, "Take heed!" It's the Bible's way of saying, "Look out!" If you think you've arrived apart from God, then grab a parachute and find the rip cord—a fall may be coming your way.

There are certain kinds of entrenched pride that only failure uproots.

Sometimes God loves us so much he'll nudge us off the edge of the altar we've erected to ourselves or to our accomplishments. We fail big-time, but that failure brings a voice that pierces our pride so we're finally able to hear. God is unrelenting in his love, and sometimes the thud from hitting bottom can actually be the sound of pride shaking loose. We may get up with our head spinning, but it's amazing how that jolt can knock the self out of our ambition.

How we respond to such a jolt is key to who we become. Os Guinness writes:

> How do we each react when we find that our noblest dreams and most profound strivings are staring in the face of failure? Never for one moment must we allow ourselves an excuse to ease up in pursuing God's call. Not for a second can we think of taking the bitter pill of apparent failure and sugarcoating it with rationalizations about the difficult times in which we live. God knew the times in which he called us to live, and he alone knows the outcome of our times as he knows the outcome of our lives and our work. Our "failures" may be his success. Our "setbacks" may prove his turning points. Our "disasters" may turn out to be his triumphs.[10]

It certainly worked this way for Brainerd. One commentator observed, "After his expulsion, he never again separated faith from practice; as a missionary, he took the precise step of putting his faith into practice."[11] Brainerd got the point: gifts and ambition don't make the man, but responding in humility to failure often does. In the unfathomable mercy of God, failure addresses not only what we're doing, but who we're becoming.

Failure is hard. There are easier ways to learn humility. But when we ignore those, God remains faithful to us, even if that means laying us low. He's a faithful Father, always helping us move faith into practice and pointing the way to the better plan.

Midnight Train Moments

We can develop some strange and faulty ideas as we go through life. We define progress as a constant ascent up the ladder of dreams. Then we fuse our joy with how much progress we're able to obtain. The mere idea of not climbing or, even worse, stepping off the ladder for a time is sheer lunacy to us. We're climbers. To stop climbing would mean we stop being who we think we are.

But God sees progress differently. To work in our souls, he occasionally pulls us aside for a little one-on-one time. It may be illness, crisis, an unexpected downsizing, an unfavorable evaluation, loving discipline from God, or a host of other reasons especially chosen for us. And the effect is always the same. We go from running full speed in a well-defined race to unexpectedly standing on the sidelines.

These times are not random. They're often preparation for a divine redirection. I think David Brainerd could relate.

> Before the way was cut off for him to the pastorate, Brainerd had no thought of being a missionary to the Indians. But now he had to rethink his whole life. There was a law, recently passed, that no established minister could be installed in Connecticut who had not graduated from Harvard, Yale, or a European university. So Brainerd felt cut off from his life calling.[12]

Have you ever felt that way? Done something dumb that permanently shut a door you felt called to walk through? Pursued something big only to meet spectacular failure? I call them "midnight train moments" after the famous Gladys Knight song:

> He kept dreamin' that someday he'd be a star,
> But he sho' found out the hard way that dreams don't always
>   come true.

So he's pawned all his hopes and he even sold his own car,
Bought a one-way ticket back to the life he once knew;
Said he's leavin' on that midnight train to Georgia,
Said he's goin' back to find the simpler place and time.[13]

Now I'm no Pip, but I know who composes the "midnight train moments" of life. Our Father has designed those times when we've thrown ourselves wholeheartedly at something, missed it, and now need an exit strategy. It's the long, lonely road back from failure. Abraham traveled it. So did Joseph. David? You bet. The great apostle Peter? Absolutely. God thinks nothing of taking our life plan, ripping it in two, and rewriting it—for our good.

When our plans lie in ruins, we know that God has a better plan. No need to pawn our hopes; we just have to invest them in a different direction and thank God for his wisdom.

The great eighteenth-century evangelist George Whitefield experienced the sting of being sidelined but also the song of trust in God. When Whitefield sustained a head injury, a younger man was called to serve in his place. Upon hearing how this man powerfully served in his absence, Whitefield rejoiced, saying, "Blessed be God that some can speak, though I am laid aside."[14]

Unsatisfied Goals

Are you an ambitious goal setter? I like goals too. Okay, I love goals. I love the feeling of striking a completed item off my to-do list. Finishing several tasks in a short period gives me the equivalent of a runner's high. It sets my endorphins dancing.

Goals may be great esteem boosters and even solid guideposts, but they also tell us something about ourselves: they reflect desires. Sometimes goals reveal a heart that understands God's Word and is ambitiously reaching for ways to glorify God. At other times, goals are a monument to an exaggerated self-assessment.

I remember starting an entry-level position in a large company. My goal—and I say this with all humility—was to be a senior executive within a year. Looking back, it would have taken a brain transplant or the sudden mass resignation of about five thousand people for me to hit that goal. It wasn't rooted in reality.

Think about the young mom who dreams of all her kids reading by three (never mind that her two-year-old isn't even walking yet), or the slacker in his late twenties who says, "I want to be a millionaire by the time I'm thirty." Or Jake, whose trifecta of goals revealed an inflated sense of selfish ambition.

Sometimes we confuse our goals with God's will.

But think about this: if we're not perfect, then our goals aren't perfect either. Sometimes we confuse our goals with God's will. We think they're the same thing. So an inevitable part of life is the frustration of at least some of our goals. We simply won't get everything we want or do everything we desire. God has a different plan than simply giving us the satisfaction of a completed to-do list. He frustrates us to change us—to turn our life in a different direction. But even more important, to bend our heart toward the habitual posture of submission and obedience. He gets us off our fast track and onto a lonely train at midnight to somewhere we didn't plan to go.

David Brainerd ran smack into his midnight train moment, and he bent his will toward God in the midst of it.

One of the things that amazes me about Brainerd is how quickly he saw the midnight train and got his ticket. I'd have been carrying a protest sign outside Yale's administration building and letting the air out of Professor Whittelsey's buggy tires until I got justice. But Brainerd bent his knee before the providence of God.

On his birthday of the same year he was expelled, Brainerd reflected on his experience. This was his conclusion: "This day I am twenty-four years of age. O how much mercy have I received the year past! How often has God *caused his goodness to pass before me!*"[15]

David Brainerd saw his failure as God's mercy. And once he saw that, he began to see a new future. His soul was anchored not to his dream but to his hope in God.

Learning the Lesson of Failure

God works in us in order to work through us. The internal work moves us to a place of peace where we come to terms with God's ability to work good even when we're bad. Resolving our regrets in light of God's goodness brings great glory to God's name.

John Piper sees that message as a prominent feature of Brainerd's failure:

> There is a tremendous lesson here. God is at work for the glory of his name and the good of his church even when the good intentions of his servants fail—even when that failing is owing to sin or carelessness. One careless word, spoken in haste, and Brainerd's life seemed to fall apart before his eyes. But God knew better, and Brainerd came to accept it.[16]

Brainerd was able to move beyond feelings of shame, anger, or self-pity to see his experience in light of God's sovereignty. That wasn't just good applied theology. It was the first marker on the road to rest and peace and the eventual purpose for which God was preparing him. The peace he sought wouldn't be discovered by raging against "the man," or playing the blame game, or wallowing in self-pity. It could be found only in what Ephesians 6:15 calls "the gospel of peace."

How did that work? That's an important question, particularly if you live haunted by some failure in your past.

The gospel reminds us that God controls all situations. If God put Pilate in power and worked through his weakness to save the world (John 19:8, 11), then Yale's review board was certainly within his jurisdiction as well. That meant Brainerd's failure and the board's rejection were not random. God controls people in power and the decisions they make, whether or not they feel God's invisible hand on their backs. And he does it by working through the desires of their heart, as Proverbs 21:1 affirms: "The king's heart is a stream of water in the hand of the LORD; he turns it wherever he will."

Brainerd concluded that his failure and the board's overreaction were God's will. Through it all, God was working some extraordinary end. Trusting God's wisdom became a place of comfort and rest despite the uncertainty of his future.

I felt myself exceeding calm, and quite resigned to God, respecting my future employment *when* and *where* he pleased: my faith lifted me above the world, and removed all those mountains, that I could not look over of late . . . I now found sweetly revived in my mind the wonderful discovery of infinite wisdom in all the dispensations of God towards me, which I had a little before I met with my great trial at college: every thing appeared full of the wisdom of God.[17]

The gospel shows us that Jesus chooses those who are failures to display his glory.

The gospel shows us that Jesus chooses those who are failures to display his glory. Peter denied Christ three times and fled from him in his moments of greatest need. He was a failure as a disciple and as a friend. The gospel makes no sense for those who don't see themselves in Peter's failure. Those who aren't failures have no need of good news. Jesus says, "Those who are well have no need of a physician, but those who are sick. I came not to call the righteous, but sinners" (Mark 2:17). We're sinners, so we fail. Jesus, the Great Physician, is the only one who never fails. Because of his death and resurrection, we're not chained to our failures.

The cross is the ultimate wisdom of God for our failures. It's God's reminder that our failures are never big enough to interrupt God's plan for our lives. For Peter, and for all of us, there's hope beyond failure. There's another chance.

I once heard a story about Thomas Edison and his team that invented the lightbulb. When it was finished, he gave it to a young boy to carry to another part of the building. You guessed it. The kid dropped the bulb. Edison was undaunted. He immediately had another made, then called the boy back, handed him the second lightbulb, and instructed him to try again. He actually gave him a second chance. I guess he made it, because I'm writing under a lightbulb right now.

The gospel announces that we're not defined by our dropped lightbulbs. There's always another chance. Because the gospel works, we can have rest.

This kind of gospel confidence inspires gospel attitudes. How do we really summon the courage to treat people kindly who have acted against us? Why not just smack them upside the head and be done with it?

Brainerd embraced the better plan. God's will became his will. His soul was at rest. Rather than being defined by his failure, he moved on. Instead of launching a campaign for vindication, he became an agent of peace. Experiencing God in that failure would transform the way he approached people and problems for the rest of his short life. Just listen:

> God has made me willing to do anything that I can do, consistent with truth, for the sake of peace, and that I might not be a stumbling block to others. For this reason I can cheerfully forego and give up what I verily believe, after the most mature and impartial search, is my right, in some instances. God has given me that disposition that, if this were the case that a man has done me an hundred injuries and I (though ever so much provoked to it) have done him one, I feel disposed and heartily willing humbly to confess my fault to him, and on my knees to ask forgiveness of him; though at the same time he should justify himself in all the injuries he has done me and should only make use of my humble confession to blacken my character the more and represent me as the only person guilty.[18]

The gospel restores God to the center of our failure analysis. God's power, love, and care become the lens through which we interpret our experience. Only from a place of peace and rest can we say of others who've humiliated us, "You meant evil against me, but God meant it for good" (Gen. 50:20).

Finding Our Definition

Failure will be an end for us if we remove God from the equation. For David Brainerd, God was very much a part of the equation. For him, another day was dawning.

Shortly after his expulsion, a group of ministers, sympathetic to Brainerd's situation, licensed him to preach. This opened the way for him to be appointed as a missionary to the Indians.

Revival wasn't immediately sparked by Brainerd's arrival on the mission field. His experience in his new calling became much like mine and yours—trial and error, discouragement, pressing on despite little fruit. Almost a year into it, Brainerd wrote this:

> As to my success here I cannot say much as yet: the Indians seem generally kind, and well-disposed towards me, and are mostly very attentive to my instructions, and seem willing to be taught further. Two or three, I hope, are under some convictions: but there seems to be little of the special workings of the divine Spirit among them yet; which gives me many a heart-sinking hour. Sometimes I hope, God has abundant blessings in store for them and me; but at other times, I am so overwhelmed with distress that I cannot see how his dealings with me are consistent with covenant love and faithfulness; and I say, "Surely his tender mercies are clean gone for ever." But however, I see, I needed all this chastisement already: "It is good for me" that I have endured these trials, and have hitherto little or no apparent success.[19]

How does a man who has gone from college expulsion to little success in service conclude, "'It is good for me' that I have endured these trials, and have little or no apparent success"? How can ambitions thrive under the cloud of indiscernible achievement? It's not a theoretical question. It's one every Christian eventually faces.

In the shadow of failure we find humbling grace. We learn that we're limited. We discover that God is more interested in who we're becoming than in what we're achieving. We find our definition not in our failures or successes but in Christ.

For David Brainerd, failure was a lesson, not a label. It didn't condemn him; it coached him. The practice of trusting God and humbling self became a paradigm for enduring future disappointments for the moments when ambitions remain unrealized. Os Guinness says it this way:

> If we define all that we are before our great Caller and live our lives before one audience—the Audience of One—then we cannot define or decide our own achievements and our own success. It is not for us to say what we have accomplished. It is not for us to pronounce ourselves successful. It is not for us to spell out what our legacy has been. Indeed, it is not even for us to know. Only the Caller can say.

Only the Last Day will tell. Only the final "Well done" will show what we have really done.[20]

Remember, we fail because we're not God. Whether it's the result of selfish ambition or the design of God for our good, failure isn't foreign. Failure is ambition refused (one way or another) for a better plan.

Brainerd persevered, and eventually God smiled upon his service: revival broke out among the Delaware Indians. God was faithful indeed.

But God's smile and his faithfulness are still there even if, in this life, we never see any fruit from our ambition being redirected by failure into God's better plan. A friend brought to my attention these words from Samuel Rutherford, who felt his earthly ministry was a complete failure: "Grace grows best in winter."

For David Brainerd, God's grace and mercy meant that his failure opened a door for new ambitions. His expulsion was God's redirection. And within a few years, one of the greatest theologians in the history of the world, Mr. Edwards himself, was publishing Brainerd's diary. And that diary, including Brainerd's account of God's dealing with him in failure, became one of the most influential tools in the history of world missions.

And on that day in heaven when Brainerd heard "Well done," I imagine him rejoicing over the Savior's power. God redeemed even his greatest mistake. His ambition was rescued when it was refused for a better plan.

9

Ambitious for the Church

AMBITION FINDS EXPRESSION IN
A SURPRISING PLACE

What would compel a man to go to the following lengths to "force" himself into a church?

> I well remember how I joined the church after my conversion. I forced myself into it by telling the minister, who was lax and slow, after I had called four or five times and could not see him, that I had done my duty. And if he did not see me, I would call a church meeting myself and tell them I believed in Christ, and ask them if they would have me.[1]

Okay, so "lax and slow" I understand. I've had more of those days than I care to admit. Just today I asked my secretary to investigate why my new cell phone hadn't been ringing for days. She asked me if the mute button was on. It was. These things come with mute buttons?

I know lax and slow.

But how do you live down almost refusing Charles Spurgeon membership in your church? (Yes, those are Spurgeon's words quoted above.) I think that's a memory you just permanently delete—then you make sure your secretary doesn't find out.

But the focus here isn't the lax and slow pastor; it's the earnest young man trying to join the church. The man who would become known as "the prince of preachers" was repeatedly rebuffed in his attempts to join a church. But Spurgeon wouldn't be deterred—and he was no fool.

You might say, "Of course Spurgeon was interested in the church.

After all, didn't he want to be a minister?" But this experience and his ambition for the church came before he ever pursued being a pastor.

When it came to the church, apparently Charles Spurgeon was neither lax nor slow. He understood something many Christians miss today: God's purpose for our ambition is connected to the local church.

It may seem as if we've taken some unexpected turns in this book in our exploration of ambition. And this may seem the oddest turn of all: I believe every Christian's ambition must include meaningful participation in the local church.

Why Is Ambition for the Church Important?

We've talked a lot in this book about aligning our ambition with God's purposes. Christ has rescued us from our lifestyle of glory-hoarding. Now we're free to prize what he values and to pursue what he treasures. So if Christ tells us what his goals are, we'd better listen up.

When we do, we discover something that might be surprising: Christ didn't come just to save sinners; he came to build a community of saved sinners. They're called the church. Ambition for the church isn't particular to Charles Spurgeon. His vision is simply an echo of the great salvation plan of the Savior.

CHRIST'S AMBITION IS FOR THE CHURCH

In Matthew 16, Jesus grants his disciples a peek into the future: "I will build my church, and the gates of hell shall not prevail against it" (v. 18).

As we read these words, we're listening in on a pivotal conversation. Peter has just made the ultimate confession on behalf of the disciples: "You are the Christ, the Son of the living God" (v. 16). In response, Jesus informs Peter that this understanding of Christ's identity was not an original thought with Peter—the heavenly Father had revealed it to him. The content of Peter's confession had colossal implications for the future of all believers. When Christ says, "I will build my church," he isn't just letting his followers in on his future plans. He's giving the resolution to the relational catastrophe that occurred way back in the fall of man.

Sin separates. That was the first and most devastating effect in Eden—alienation from God followed by conflict between man and woman. Sin corrupts creation and destroys relationships. But the Old Testament resounds with the promise that division and estrangement would not always define God's people: "This is the covenant that I will make with the house of Israel after those days, declares the LORD: I will put my law within them, and I will write it on their hearts. And I will be their God, and they shall be my people" (Jer. 31:33).

In other words, a new covenant was coming, one that would restore us to God and bind us to one another in love and truth. Those set apart to experience this supernatural grace would be called "my people"—the church. This is the promise Christ is fulfilling when he says, "I will build my church."

So the church represents Christ's reconciled people. As we live in community, we exalt Christ's purposes. Though sin once isolated us, the cross now unifies us. As citizens of a new kingdom and members of the household of God (Eph. 2:19), we're no longer merely individuals, concerned only with ourselves. We're now "a chosen race, a royal priesthood, a holy nation, a people for his own possession" (1 Pet. 2:9). We're the church universal, the sum total of all the redeemed everywhere for all time.

The individual Christian simply cannot understand his ambition in purely individual terms.

Christ's promise introduces us to a radical, countercultural idea: the satisfaction of individual ambition is linked to our collective identity as the people of God. The individual Christian simply cannot understand his purpose, and therefore his ambition, in purely individual terms.

This community Christ is building is something he *loves*—and not in a merely abstract way. He cherishes it as a husband cherishes his wife. He prizes it as his greatest possession. And he pursues it, even to the point of sacrificing his own life for the church—for us.

If Christ displayed such a love and ambition for the church, shouldn't we also? Should we not prize and pursue that which Jesus himself prizes and pursues? Shouldn't our ambition be modeled after his?

Sure, we say, but what does this look like on the ground? The reality of the universal church is a wonderful, profound truth. It is glorious and grand. And it's easy to let it stay out there with all those other great, inspiring, abstract ideas, like justice, beauty, the well-behaved child, and the empty in-box. But Christ is talking about real people, in real community. That's why we must move beyond abstraction and learn to love a *specific local church*.

Simply put, anyone who claims to be a part of the universal church must express that identification in a local church community. Edmund Clowney describes the local church this way: "The church is the form that Christ has appointed for the community of those who confess his name; in the church alone, the body of Christ is made visible in this world."[2]

Suppose I told you I love Scotland. In fact, I love Scotland so much that I change my name to Dave McHarvey, begin speaking in a rich Scottish brogue, wear a kilt, and learn to play the bagpipes at parties. My friends might suspect I've left earth for unknown planets, but it's no matter to me, I love Scotland.

Naturally you would ask me, "So how many times have you been to Scotland?"

"I've never actually been there," I reply. "But I've heard a lot about it and read about it. I'm really quite fond of it."

"Do you have friends who are Scottish?"

"Not exactly, but I hear they're cool."

"Have you ever done anything for the Scottish people?"

"Nope, never had time. Life's busy. Besides, my love for Scotland is a private, personal thing. It exists in my heart. I don't ask anything of any Scots, and they don't require anything of me. Things would get too complicated if I had to deal with the people. I just love the idea of Scotland!"

There's no way you'd agree I had a genuine love for Scotland. Yet it's not uncommon for Christians to speak in a similar manner about their love for the church, their belief in the church, even the priority of the church—all while having little to no meaningful involvement with the church.

The reality is, the only way we can express a love for the universal church is to be tangibly involved in the local church. Yep, that might mean the church you're thinking about right now, the one that meets in an old brick building or the local school's gym, where the people can sometimes be a little annoying and the music too loud. A local church.

Those very people—the Christians in your town who sometimes delight and sometimes annoy you—are part of what Christ is talking about when he says, "I will build my church." If our ambition is to align with Christ's, we must be ambitious for our local church.

OUR AMBITION FOR THE CHURCH IS TOO OFTEN "LAX AND SLOW"

When I was growing up, my neighborhood was a community. If I did something wrong, I was yelled at by six neighbors before going home to be yelled at by my parents. But I knew they were all looking out for me. I was one of them, and they wanted to make sure I stayed that way. One time a neighborhood mom talked the police out of taking me away because of some, umm, "mischief." Her reasoning was unassailable; I was "one of the neighborhood boys." (And she didn't even like me.)

Things nowadays are different. Our sense of community has been largely lost, or maybe overwhelmed by the power of self. We're a culture committed to self-fulfillment, self-expression, self-esteem, self-preservation—self, self, self. "To a great majority of Americans," says David Wells, "self has become the source of all values. The pursuit of self is what life is all about."[3]

The pursuit of self-spirituality has replaced the idea of Christianity in community.

The church didn't escape the tornado of individualism that swept through our world. The winds of "I, me, and mine" pummeled evangelicalism, leaving a landscape of private, personal, customized faith. The pursuit of self-spirituality—a highly personalized vision for religious quest—replaced the idea of Christianity in community.

This sets us up for the mirage of virtual community. The virtual community in its rapidly mutating forms feeds on self in two ways: it's a logical outlet for individual spirituality and also a primary shaper in how we view relationships with others. In the online world it's possible to have at least some sense of what we call "church." We can listen to the best sermons on the planet, listen and sing to cutting-edge worship music, share our spiritual experiences, organize our religious activities—all without ever getting out of bed. In fact, the only things that have yet to be replicated online are the fundamental sacraments of baptism and the Lord's Supper, though I'm sure somebody somewhere is trying to figure that out.

Last summer we rented a place at the beach for a few weeks, and I did some writing there. While there, I met a Christian surfer who invited me to a surfers' Bible study on the beach. It was cool—and the first time I ever heard the word *gnarly* used in a message. About forty or so young people were there, turning out to study God's Word. That was truly gnarly, but was it a local church?

Today many groups unite around a common interest, sprinkle in some Scripture, and view it as their church. My surfer Bible study was a mixed bag. Some were involved in local churches and saw this as a great way to connect with other surfer believers and reach out. But I know that for a few there, this was their "church."

I think that happens a lot today for some believers. Rather than fostering a Christianity lived out in the church, some Christians unintentionally replace the church and encourage detachment. That's not biblical Christianity. And it's certainly not gnarly.

An individualized faith makes us "lax and slow" regarding the local church. We're like choir members who don't see any real point in actually standing together and singing the same music. Instead we mill about, occasionally forming duets or trios, but the power and passion of the entire ensemble is never heard. And the cause of Christ suffers for it. Joshua Harris calls it "dating the church."[4] Donald Whitney calls those who do it "spiritual hitchhikers"; they want "all the benefits but no responsibility; all take and no give; no accountability, just a free ride."[5] They're really just drifting.

As a pastor, I've seen my share of spiritual hitchhikers. My heart always goes out to them. Bundled with dreams but lacking Christ's ambition for the church, they're ever traveling, never building.

It's not that their lives don't bear fruit. Trees can bear fruit under all kinds of conditions. My neighbor once planted a fig tree in the only small patch of dirt available on our shared driveway. It spit figs on my car like an old trucker with a good dip. Trees and Christians share that similarity—they can bear fruit in almost any space. But the most fruitful Christian life is one spent loving the local church.

The New Testament declares the essential place of the local church in the Christian life:

- The very first believers "devoted themselves to the apostles' teaching and the fellowship, to the breaking of bread and the prayers. . . . And all who believed were *together*" (Acts 2:42, 44).
- Teaching and preaching were experienced publicly. Timothy, as a pastor, was commanded to devote himself "to the *public* reading of Scripture, to exhortation, to teaching" (1 Tim. 4:13).
- Believers were exhorted "to meet together . . . encouraging one another" (Heb. 10:25).
- They were repeatedly called to "serve one another" (Gal. 5:13; 1 Pet. 4:10).

All this was possible because Christ's passion became their ambition. People gather around their passions. If our passion is the church, the church is where we'll gather.

Join the Church Jesus Loves

It's no secret that churches are filled with sinners. Yep, it's true. Your pastor, a sinner. Your Sunday school teacher or small group leader, a sinner. The person writing this book and the one reading it, both sinners. Though redeemed by saving grace, the church won't be perfect, because it's a community of sinners. As you apply your ambition to be part of a local church, you can be sure you'll see flaws.

But that's not the point, is it? Ambition for the church compels us to join our imperfect self with other imperfect selves to form an imperfect community—all for the glory of God.

If you're already a part of a local church, I want to commend you for that. But if you're like one of my surfer friends who has an epiphany as he's carving an epic wave—"Dude, I gotta find a church!"—let me offer some brief pastoral advice for what to look for in a church you would consider joining.

What are the church's values and vision? What does the church teach? Is it sound, biblical doctrine? Is the gospel at the heart of what the church is about? And how is this doctrine applied in the church's values and vision? Does the church practice what it preaches?

When we join a church, we don't join a static organization. We join a people heading in a direction. It's good to know what that direction is.

How is the church pastored and governed? Is the governing structure of the church one that can be supported by the Scriptures? Are the leaders (elders or pastors) qualified to hold the positions they have, based on the biblical qualifications found in 1 Timothy 3:1–7 and Titus 1:5–9? Are the teaching, preaching, and pastoral care of the church done with faithful and gracious application rooted in the hope of the gospel and consistent with God's Word?

Our lives are profoundly influenced by the leaders of our churches. Our confidence is in God, but we should also have confidence in his delegated leadership.

Is there true fellowship among the people? Do you see evidence that membership in the church goes beyond attendance at meetings and acts of service? Though these are important, church membership should lead to developing relationships and deepening fellowship. Each person should find a spiritual family and home in the church (Heb. 10:24–25).

Does the gospel move the church toward those outside the church? A great evidence of a good church is that they see beyond themselves. We don't turn inward and construct church cocoons. Nope, the Great Commission is real, it's potent, and it moves us toward the lost.

Those are four ways we ask visitors to evaluate our church. Notice that a lot of things we might think are important—size, worship style, socioeconomic makeup, denominational affiliation—don't make it high on the list. I'm just trying to keep it simple for all you surfer dudes out there.

Build the Church Jesus Loves

Just adding our names to a church's membership roster isn't sufficient. A holy ambition for the church finds delight in *building* it. Joining is the entrance to the freeway, not the rest stop.

When the Lord said, "I will build my church," it wasn't just flowery prose. Jesus was announcing an extraordinary ambition—to remain devoted to his church and our endurance in it. His ambition must inspire our action. Being added to a church should mean we're serving, sacrificing, sharing, connecting . . . *living* in a way that augments the strength and health of the church.

In today's affluent societies, the church faces different challenges than the churches did in the New Testament. Persecution for us doesn't come in a threat of death but in the trauma of someone not liking us because we're Christians. It's when coworkers don't invite us to hang out after work.

The real danger most of us face today is not persecution but distraction. As John Piper said, "There is a great gulf between the Christianity that wrestles with whether to worship at the cost of imprisonment and death, and the Christianity that wrestles with whether the kids should play soccer on Sunday morning."[6] Sometimes that great gulf swallows our ambition to build the church.

Let's face it. Even committed, longtime church members can become lax and slow in their ambition for building the church. When church is not an ambition but only a place, the real ambitions of our lives inevitably crowd it out.

There's nothing better to set your ambitions to than building a good church.

There are a lot of good things Christians can build—good families, businesses, reputations, houses, memories, lifestyles. But there's nothing better to set your ambitions to than building a good church. "Ambition that centers on the glory of God and welfare of the church," says J. Oswald Sanders, "is a mighty force for good."[7]

So does your involvement in your church contribute to its welfare? Do you help strengthen your church, or are you just another body that shows up on Sunday mornings? Is Sunday morning the day you get to gather with God's people to celebrate what he's doing and to hear what he's saying? Or is it the day you have to get up too early, drive too far, sit too long, hear too much, then try to make it back home before the game kicks off or before the meat overcooks?

The church is "the pillar and foundation of the truth" (1 Tim. 3:15, NIV) in our world and the center of God's redemptive activity. It's the one human institution that will shine brightly throughout eternity.

If we're going to build, let's build the church.

Commit to the Church Jesus Loves

Have you ever met someone whose face was split with a smile because of how long they'd been members in their church? I've met some in my travels. In fact, we have some in our church. In fact, I'm one of them. I've known only two churches in my entire Christian life, and the current one has been my home for twenty-five years. I'm smiling even as I write this.

But apparently my experience isn't the norm. It was recently reported that "Protestants are about as likely to be loyal to their toothpaste or bathroom tissue as they are to their denomination."[8] I must confess I'm glad no member of my church has expressed their loyalty in those terms—"Dave, I just want you to know, this church means even more to me than my toothpaste." Gee, thanks. I wonder if there are some who like their church *less* than their toothpaste but *more* than their toilet paper? Seriously, it's tragic if our brand loyalty trumps our loyalty to the people of God.

For a church to go forward, its members must be ambitious to commit to it over time. But commitment like this isn't popular in our consumer culture. It's not just that we're mobile and therefore apt to move around more. There's been a fundamental change in the way we relate to institutions. We see it in marriage, in the workplace, in friendships, and in how we spend our money. Sadly, we also see it vividly in the church. Choice and need have replaced sacrifice and faithfulness. The migration of believers from one church to the next has become common and expected. David Wells describes the situation: "Commitment—actual commitment, real bonds, a real sense of belonging, not just the *idea* of commitment—has become a precious stone, rare, much sought after and, when found, treasured."[9]

I want to be careful here. I realize that if you use the evaluation criteria I suggested above for finding a church to join, you might find your local church lacking in some significant ways. If that's the case, please consider talking graciously with your church leaders to see if they think these issues are important. I'm acutely aware of where my own church needs to grow and change. It benefits me, as a pastor, to have faithful church members communicate where we might do better, especially in areas where our proclamation and application of the gospel are concerned.

If you're in a church where the gospel is not central and biblical doctrine and practice are not pursued, perhaps you should consider finding a more biblically founded church. But please don't be divisive or rebellious toward those who lead the church or who want to remain there. Division in the church and disrespect of church leadership are roundly condemned in the Scriptures (1 Cor. 1:10; 3:3; 11:18–23; Titus 3:10; 1 Thess. 5:12) and must not find their way into our words or actions.

But I'm going to assume your church, while not perfect, is solid and deserves your biblical commitment. You see, every believer eventually begins to ask, "Should I stay or should I go?" These are the defining moments in church membership.

When a culture moves self to the center, ambitions entrench in the individual, not in the church.

Churches change and grow over time, which is exactly what they should do. Some churches even go through significant upheaval. There isn't a church mentioned in the New Testament that didn't know some problem testing its members. My church is much different in size and feel than when I first came. Same gospel—different programs, needs, and priorities. Challenges and changes like this should not constitute an automatic call from God to leave.

Unfortunately, it's here in our church commitment where selfish ambition can do real damage. John Calvin once wrote, "Ambition has been, and still is, the mother of all errors, of all disturbances and sects."[10] This is a provocative statement we should ponder. Calvin in his day saw selfish ambition as the origin of errors, church conflicts, and people separating. How much more that must be true in today's culture of self. When a culture moves self to the center, ambitions entrench in the individual, not in the church. "My need" becomes the rising sun that shrivels and scorches "our church" until it's brittle and lifeless.

When personal ambitions are frustrated in a church, Christians tend to either depart or drift. We need to fight against both tendencies.

I'm not saying you should stay in a dying church out of blind devotion to an institution. I'm talking about a heart posture that sees beyond the end of some tradition you hold dear, or the departure of a favorite leader, or the failure of a church to go a direction you think it should. I'm talking about impassioned devotion to remain in a gospel-centered church that's so cutting-edge it loves the old, old story. A church humble enough to be *semper reformanda*—always being reformed by the Spirit. I'm talking about a vision for local church longevity. One that sees membership as more than "meeting my needs" or "petting my doctrine"; one with a burning passion to bring the lost and the next generation into the gospel, then into the church.

Remain in the Church Jesus Loves

There's a disease infecting believers in many churches. When it goes undetected, it often results in disappointed believers departing for greener pastures. It's called My-Church-Is-for-My-Ministry. The church *is* for ministry, but this infection carries the deadly "me" virus. Once we ingest it, what we do becomes more important than what we believe or where we are.

The psalmist discovered something eternally precious: "For a day in your courts is better than a thousand elsewhere. I would rather be a doorkeeper in the house of my God than dwell in the tents of wickedness" (Ps. 84:10). A day in the right house is better than three years anywhere else. And being a lowly doorkeeper in the house of God is better than position or comforts elsewhere. I heard one guy capture the point well: "What you're a part of is more important than the part you play."

Shifting the accent from "my part" to "what I'm a part of" stirs ambition for the church. Free from the tyranny of managing the me-maniac, we can savor the fruit that accompanies the doorkeeper's devotion: first in, last to leave.

When their personal ambitions are frustrated in one church, Christians turn to another for a better bargain. But life's never easier when there's no ambition to hang on and hang around.

I thought about that when I read Randy's letter. Randy was a member of our church for several years. He was also a student at a local seminary. Randy had dreams for impact, and he was anxious to see his gifts applied to those dreams. He joined our church, but as time went on he felt his gifts were undervalued and his ambitions would never be satisfied there. So he did what seemed right in light of his personal vision. He left.

Ten years later, an envelope was sitting on my desk with the following letter inside. Randy encouraged me to freely use it as a lesson for others.

Dear Dave,

This letter is my heartfelt apology to you and the other leaders at the church. . . . Perhaps it may be of use to help someone else.

I attended the church all during my first year of seminary. I attended the special events, the commitment classes, the leadership opportunities, the evangelism training, the small groups, etc. In my mind I was sold out. In reality . . . ?

The next year, when it was time to do my pastoral internship for seminary, the leaders at church felt I should wait on God's timing to raise me up. In retrospect it was godly advice. Yet my response was not to wait. Instead I felt hurt and grieved over their decision. I now see it was my own pride and nothing else that caused me to leave the fellowship.

One year later my wife became involved with someone else, and I became a senior in seminary, a single parent to a seven-year-old daughter, and we eventually divorced. What a time in my life to be without real community and fellowship.

I now pastor a small rural church. God is having to cram life lessons in me that I should have learned years ago. It is not often pleasant, but I'm grateful that he has never abandoned me, and I'm learning how to embrace the pain and accept his faithful afflictions.

I am now remarried to a godly woman and we have two other children. In my first year and a half here as pastor, we grew to about ninety folks. It took about two years for people to really grasp the concept of commitment to Christ as expressed through commitment to fellowship. But now people understand, and we have settled in at about forty folks. Only by God's miracles of provision are we surviving.

I recently had to ask one of our small group leaders to step down. He was "lording his authority over the flock." It was and is still a sad time, since this brother is my friend and we "ache" for the lack of servant/leaders here. My friend and his wife have chosen to leave the fellowship rather than work it out. I am now ministering to his small group and others hurt by the effects of unbridled ego in leadership. And, I see now firsthand the wisdom of the leaders in the church to ask me to "wait on God to raise me up." I am certain they saved the flock there much pain that would have been caused at the expense of my ego.

So, guys, thanks for exercising wisdom. I apologize to you. I am sorry for my pride which prevented me from seeing your motivation. I'm sorry for my arrogance. I am sorry for the accusations I made. I am sorry for the lack of trust I put in God to speak correction into my life through you. But most of all, I'm sorry for the friendships in Christ with you and others that I have missed by not waiting.

With sincere humility, I ask for your forgiveness.

What a delight it was to write Randy back, extend my forgiveness, and communicate my deepest respect for his honesty and humility. But I've never forgotten his regret for how selfish ambition stole precious years and fruit from his life. In mercy God rescued Randy and his ambition, but he would want me to offer his example as a warning to others. Maybe to you.

Fighting the Tendency to Drift

For many of us, departing a church is a little too radical. We have relationships to keep, kids in youth group, a good thing going overall.

Maybe we were once at the center of the action in the church. What we said had influence. Maybe we were leaders. The church needed our gifts and talents. But now? There are new folks, and they seem to get the attention. The new singer who can actually read music. The better organizer. The guy with the Bible degree. The church no longer does the things we're good at or for which we have vision. Now we're just "one of the folks." Yet we don't want to pull up stakes and go—after all, why take the risk of starting all over? So we just drift, going with the flow.

It's a flow that will inevitably take us to the fringe of the church—out beyond where we should be.

The writer of Hebrews comes at drift pretty hard: "And let us consider how to stir up one another to love and good works, not neglecting to meet together, as is the habit of some, but encouraging one another, and all the more as you see the Day drawing near" (10:24–25). This writer is concerned that over time, some are growing cold to the church and its meetings. They neglect meeting together. Drifting toward the fringe becomes a habit. So everything in this exhortation works against drift. This passage commands us to cultivate other habits to fight the tendency to drift. In view of eternal realities, we need to draw toward the church even more, not less.

Drifters don't always know they're drifting.

Drifters don't always know they're drifting. Like the person at the beach floating on the raft, unaware the tide is taking him out to sea, we don't see what's happening. So we need each other. We need to stir up one another to love and good works, and to encourage one another, and to sharpen our shared commitment with a vision for the eternal value of the church of which we're a part.

"The Church is essential to the Christian," Elton Trueblood says, "not because it brings him personal advancement or even inspiration, but because, with all its failures, it is an indispensable instrument for the redemption of the world."[11] Whenever something or someone we love fails us, we experience that failure as a deep pain. If we love the church dearly, we'll be hurt when it fails. And it will fail. If you're in a church for any length of time, you'll experience its failure and weakness. It won't live up to what it promises. Trusted leaders will make mistakes. Ministries we devote our lives to keeping afloat may be cut because of budget or other priority concerns. Someone we love leaves the church.

What rescues true ambition for the church is not the quality of the organization or the maturity of the people. The church belongs to Jesus Christ. It is *his* great ambition. And because we're committed to Christ, it should be our great ambition as well.

Crossing the Finish Line Together

Charles Spurgeon, who led thousands to love Christ and his church, once said, "Failure at a crucial moment may mar the entire outcome of a life."[12] If the church is the stage where the Christian life is acted out, then life's "crucial moments" are the defining points where godly ambition is fed and selfish ambition frustrated.

As Christians, we can't avoid these moments. They often come as tests—pass or fail. Selfish ambition *will* contest your ambition for the church. In those crucial moments, the outcome of a life is being forged.

I know because I've been there. I've heard the roar of my own selfish ambition demanding to be fed. But God is bigger than my sin, and he's committed to pointing me in the right direction. It's his power that energizes us to serve the ambition of Christ—his church.

The church is not meant to be an earthly Utopia, nor should it be confused with heaven. Rather, we're called to honestly acknowledge and grow through the problems of church life—the imperfections, the offenses, the misunderstandings, and the glorious mission opportunities as well.

Our ambition should be higher than crossing the finish line alone. This race started when God joined us with his people. Let's finish it the same way we started: together, in his church, for the glory of God.

10

Ambitious Risk

AMBITION NEEDS RISK TO PRODUCE REWARD

I love having heroes. Not the comic book, superhuman, special powers types, but the everyday garden variety. Forget the capes or Saturday morning cartoons. I'm talking plain ole folks with plenty of grit who pursue godly ambitions—sometimes even at great risk—in obscurity. These people never show up in biographies, so one of my goals is to introduce you to some heroes I know, to make their example our inspiration.

Do you know what a foster parent is? Picture a titanium-enforced heart miraculously bent toward the needs of desperate kids. Now wrap that in skin and add a stamina package allowing him or her to survive long nights with little sleep. That's a foster parent. The ones I know are heroes-on-call, accepting spontaneous parenting assignments that would reduce Batman to a babbling bat-fool cowering in his bat-cave. If "ambition to care" were an Olympic competition, these folks would sweep all the medals.

Bob and Joanne Fannon are foster parents. Instant heroes in my book. But they carry a unique ambition. Bob and Joanne feel called to take in children whose medical conditions make them difficult to place. In their words, they take the "medically fragile" or "the neediest of the needy." So we're already in hall of fame territory here. But the story I'm going to tell you goes even further.

Ambitious to Care

While on vacation in 1997, Joanne received a call from their foster parent agency asking if they'd be interested in "a transplant child." Joanne didn't know what that meant, but she informed her husband,

Bob. As they began to pray, they sensed a distinct prompting from God to take the child, transplant and all.

The little boy's name was Christopher. Bob and Joanne contacted the agency and agreed to take him sight unseen. But the doctors insisted they visit the boy right away because Christopher had some unusual medical problems. Bob and Joanne traveled to the hospital wondering why the doctors sounded so foreboding.

The first glimpse was shocking. Christopher lived in a glass bubble. His entire world was composed of a steel cage-like crib and three life-support systems. The equipment attached to his little body was popping, hissing, and beeping—sad reminders that Christopher's life was maintained by machinery. He was now eighteen months old and had lived only two weeks of his life outside a hospital. They could see scars covering his body—a visual catalog of his suffering since birth.

Joanne instinctively turned away, her mind racing with the implications of risk in accepting Christopher as their own. The medical complications were way beyond anything she and Bob had ever encountered.

The doctors had actually placed Christopher's intestines outside his body to help them function better. There were also problems with his liver and other complications. Each time one issue was resolved, another would emerge. And now he needed transplants—if he didn't get them in time, he wouldn't live beyond the age of five.

Christopher needed round-the-clock care by people who knew how to care for this condition. Bob and Joanne knew they were unqualified—they weren't medical professionals, and they'd had no training. They had no idea what they were doing.

But they had something else—the gospel of Jesus Christ and a burning ambition to help kids who seemed hopeless.

"We were terrified and overwhelmed," Joanne recalls. "Our minds were racing—*How do we get out of this?* But as we looked at Christopher, God gave us the grace to see not only IV poles, but the life of a child, our child. And we knew that God had supplied faith for the risks up front. For us, it was a win-win."

Bob and Joanne exchanged knowing glances. Christopher had just found a home.

The Fannons had a godly ambition to care for those who desperately needed them. God had placed vision and faith deep in their hearts. As time went on, they were able to inspire faith in their other kids for this calling. They knew God called them, as a family, to care for kids in this way—to take them, love them, and share with them the glorious news of Jesus. This sense of calling formed a powerful impulse that has, over the years, filled their house with foster kids.

Following God's call involves a great deal of risk—all the time. That's something the Fannons had to accept as they pursued their godly ambition. Shortly after adopting Christopher, they received a beautiful special-needs baby named Samantha. Due to medical complications, doctors predicted she would live only into her thirties. However, soon after she came to the Fannons, it was discovered that her body was riddled with cancer. As she fought for her life, the Fannons lavished their love on her. She was officially adopted into their family just hours before she died at the age of three.

This is holy ground kind of stuff. Radical love. Risky love.

Taking risks in foster care or adoptions hardly makes headlines. Risk is something we commercialize by removing it from routine life and assigning it to high-profile stuff like business or extreme sports. We take political risks, financial risks, mission risks, business risks, and even safety risks. But risks of the heart or home don't seem to get airtime. It's a shame, because that's where most of life is lived, and that's where ambitions often become reality. Ambition isn't something that waits for the big promotion.

The Fannons started right where they were, and they accepted an important reality. Where there's ambition, there must be risk. Risk is the cost of ambition.

Sharing Paul's Risks

When God speaks, you have two options.

You can flee in an attempt to protect yourself from the risk of obedience. Jonah tried that. But God loves us too much to approve our exit strategy. Jonah eventually understood that, but not before spending three nights in Hotel Humpback.

The second option is to move forward in faith, not dismissing the risk, but accepting it as part of the path. This is what Bob and Joanne did in opening their home to Christopher. They were moved by the claim the gospel made on them, and they embraced the accompanying risks.

They're not alone. The gospel made audacious claims upon Paul many centuries before.

We see it especially in Acts 20. As Paul was on his way to Jerusalem, his ship was docked in Miletus, about thirty miles from the church he'd helped establish in Ephesus. Paul had a lot of history with the elders of the Ephesian church, so knowing his mates were nearby, he called for them. He wanted to pass along some things that might help them in their ambition to preach the gospel and build the church.

Here's what he told them:

> You yourselves know how I lived among you the whole time from the first day that I set foot in Asia, serving the Lord with all humility and with tears and with trials that happened to me through the plots of the Jews; how I did not shrink from declaring to you anything that was profitable, and teaching you in public and from house to house, testifying both to Jews and to Greeks of repentance toward God and of faith in our Lord Jesus Christ. And now, behold, I am going to Jerusalem, constrained by the Spirit, not knowing what will happen to me there, except that the Holy Spirit testifies to me in every city that imprisonment and afflictions await me. But I do not account my life of any value nor as precious to myself, if only I may finish my course and the ministry that I received from the Lord Jesus, to testify to the gospel of the grace of God. And now, behold, I know that none of you among whom I have gone about proclaiming the kingdom will see my face again. (vv. 18–25)

I'm no Paul; my life is complicated enough just being Dave. And we must all approach Paul's ministry and example remembering the big differences between him and us. For example, Paul went to "the third heaven" (2 Cor. 12:2). That's something I never accomplished, even when I dabbled in drugs. Paul had unprecedented insight into the gospel and a unique call to the Gentiles. Paul was in a league of his own, and none of us plays ball there.

But we can appreciate some important similarities between Paul and ourselves. For instance, we carry the same gospel Paul carried. I love the way Charles Spurgeon's grandfather put it when commenting on his grandson's gifting: "He may preach the gospel better than I do, but he does not preach a better gospel."[1] Paul was a better gospel preacher than any of us, but he didn't preach a better gospel. That's something worth pondering.

> We carry the same gospel Paul carried,
> and it requires us to have a similar ambition.

We also share another similarity with Paul. Not only do we have the same gospel Paul carried, but the spread of that gospel requires us to have a similar ambition to Paul's, and to take similar risks. I don't mean we'll all end up in prison, as Paul did. But it takes risk and sacrifice for the gospel to move forward. In that sense, the gospel makes the same claim upon us it did upon Paul.

The Audacious Claim

The unstoppable gospel requires a fierce ambition to put it into play. Paul said, "I make it my ambition to preach the gospel, not where Christ has already been named" (Rom. 15:20). For Paul to get the gospel to new places and new people, he had to "make it [his] ambition."

Having an ambition for the gospel pushes us to do things we never expected. It incites us to look beyond the borders of our comfort and convenience. The gospel stokes ambition by making audacious claims upon it.

Audacious hardly brings to mind serenity or comfort. Nobody ever claims to have an audacious sleep or an audacious moment of poetry reading. Nope, to be audacious is to be bold or daring, fearless, courageous, intrepid, dauntless, venturesome. That's wild stuff—the kind of stuff making risky adoptions possible. It's also the kind of stuff defining Paul's life.

Not all of us are called to risk our lives like Paul or to adopt high-risk kids like the Fannons. In fact, I'm not even trying to compare Paul's risk with the Fannons' risk. Audacious risk can be expressed in diverse ways by *both* the extraordinary Paul and the ordinary Bob and Joanne—that's what keeps the attention off risk-takers and on the reason for their risk.

God has designed the mission in a way that the gospel goes forward only through risk, cost, and sacrifice—be it to Rome, to rural America, or to Ricky in the next cubicle at work. Ambition and risk are the human ingredients God uses to put the gospel into circulation.

Here's where we discover a strange irony. God wants to rescue ambition so that ambition, in turn, can rescue us. Ambition rescues us by exerting claims on us that change our lives.

Claim One: Step Out beyond the Known

Ambition rescues us from misplaced security.

Bob and Joanne stepped into a future filled with uncertainty. Would Christopher live? Would they have the ability to care for him? What toll would his condition take on the family? They could explore these questions with unceasing prayer and faithfulness, but they would never truly know what the future would hold. They could plan and prepare, and they did, but they couldn't protect themselves from the unknowns surrounding Christopher's future and condition. They were stepping way beyond what they knew.

Paul could certainly relate. Stepping beyond the known was an experience that began at his conversion.

That conversion itself was unconventional. Knocked off his horse, miraculously blinded, hearing a personal accusation from God—not stuff you'd want to stand up and testify about at the next baptism. But the fun didn't end there. Jesus closes out their little confrontation on the road by saying, "Rise and enter the city, and you will be told what you are to do" (Acts 9:6). In that simple directive, a vast reorientation program had begun. Paul would be fired with ambitions to take the gospel to faraway lands. But he would also learn an important lesson: ambitions can be godly only if they're dependent.

So God began a divine routine: he would give Paul direction but withhold the outcome. If Paul had a bumper sticker, it would read, "Going, not knowing."

The routine appears in Acts 13. Prophets and teachers were gathered in the church at Antioch. "While they were worshiping the Lord and fasting, the Holy Spirit said, 'Set apart for me Barnabas and Saul for the work to which I have called them'" (v. 2). Note that God never specifies the work. He just asks that these two men be set apart and sent out. As for any questions about direction and destination—he'd have to get back to them on that.

In Acts 16 the uncertainty routine continues. Paul is on his way somewhere else when he has a dream: "A man of Macedonia was standing there, urging him and saying, 'Come over to Macedonia and help us'" (v. 9). If that were me, I'd be saying, "Helpful, but can we get some additional information, Lord? An address, maybe a name, a decent hotel recommendation perhaps? After all, Macedonia is a big place." But God doesn't fill in those blanks at first. He gives Paul enough answers to stir his ambition but never enough to mute his faith.

This brings us back to Paul in Miletus, talking with the Ephesian church elders. He tells them, "And now, behold, I am going to Jerusalem, constrained by the Spirit, not knowing what will happen to me there, except that the Holy Spirit testifies to me in every city that imprisonment and afflictions await me" (Acts 20:22–23). It's the same routine: God constrains Paul to go but withholds what will happen. Paul has an ambition and is going forward, but he doesn't foresee the outcome. His only certainty is that it's risky. He's going, not knowing.

I used to hike with my kids to plumb life's deeper questions. That's what put me five miles up a trail at a lookout known as the Pinnacle with my oldest son on a sparkling fall day. As we sat enjoying the view, some college students invited us to explore a nearby cave. So life found me that day crawling in a cave behind a group of guys I'd never met, to a place I'd never been, for an activity I'd never done. It was awesome.

Soon we came to an open chamber where sunlight shone down through a hole in the cave ceiling. The hole was just about big enough for someone to squeeze through. While I stood marveling at the whole setup, the college students began to climb the cave wall to exit through the ceiling hole. I now understood this was why they were there. That wasn't so awesome because I also understood where this whole thing was going.

My son exploded in enthusiasm. As the last student disappeared through the ceiling, he turned and pleaded, "Aw, come on, Dad. Can I please go up the cave wall? Please?" I tried to explain that his mother sent us off together that morning, and it would create real problems if I came home alone.

But that didn't seem to help. So I thought to myself, *Dave, you're here to build a memory. Kimm is ninety miles away. She doesn't need to know the details. Percentages are in your favor that the kid won't kill himself.*

"Oh, go on son," I exclaimed. "Climb the wall!"

With little effort, he scampered up the cave wall and out the top. Problem solved. No bloodshed. Memory made. Let's roll. Where's that tunnel out of here?

But my new college buddies had something else in mind. "Come on up!" they called through the hole. "It'll be fun." *Fun?* The whole thing sounded like lunacy to me. College students have no idea how your definition of fun changes once you have a wife, four kids, a mortgage, and a temperamental back. Scaling cave walls no longer qualified as fun—it was bumped off the list by a little something called sanity.

So I waved them off.

Later, silently walking back down the trail with my son, I suddenly felt very old. Ancient actually. I felt like someone should just wrap me in a blanket and feed me prunes. My son's disappointment was palpable, shadowing my every step. But no worries. I told myself that disappointment passes, while the pain of falling off cave walls remains for a long time.

But the inner ego couldn't be silenced. "Son," I shouted, "I'm going back!" Suddenly I felt like a Viking or something. I knew it was the right decision when my son said, "Yes!"—as if to say, "My dad's *not* a wimp."

Fifteen minutes later I was studying the wall to plot my ascent. Now I should probably say that I don't think this was a particularly dangerous climb, but none of that mattered to me. It was my first climb, and for a first-time climber every cave wall is Mount Everest. At least that's my theory. Anyway, things seemed to be going well— meaning I hadn't killed myself yet—when I reached a ledge. To finish the climb, I had to push off from it so my hand and foot could catch a ledge on the adjacent wall. If properly executed, I would then be straddling the cave chamber, hands pressed against the two opposite cave walls. Unflattering, yes, but necessary.

Well you guessed it. Dave-the-Sherpa missed the ledge. My foot began sliding down the side of the cave wall. The good news was I no longer felt old. My muscles locked down, and my foot hit an elevated bump, stopping the slide.

Minds do funny things in those moments where there's risk in every motion. "Hey, this cave climate ain't bad. Maybe I could stay here. Maybe I could live here! Yeah, Kimm could bring the kids and some food. We'd be warm and dry. They could even decorate me for Christmas."

Nope, I thought, *not possible.* I couldn't stay where I was, nor was there any going back. The only place to go was forward and upward—yet doing so placed me at great risk.

God puts us where we feel compelled to climb despite the risks.

God moves in our lives in a similar way. He puts us where we feel compelled to climb despite the risks. We don't know what's through the hole; we don't know whether our foot will slip. Advancing may be costly. To move at all seems risky. Yet we can't stop; we feel compelled to press ahead.

The Christian life is a kind of mysterious suspense, where we're acting on godly ambition without knowing the result. Like Paul, we're "going to Jerusalem, constrained by the Spirit, not knowing what will happen."

Oh, and by the way, I'll hold you in suspense no longer—I did not die.

THE RESCUE OF RISK

Risks and uncertainty are daily reminders of how much greater God is than we are. We take risks; God does not. God is not "going" (because he's already there), nor is he "not knowing" (since he knows all things). God is all-powerful, controlling all things. Amazing, isn't it? God is right now spinning the entire universe like a basketball on his big finger and at the same time controlling the amount of times you blink as you're reading this paragraph.

Risk happens because we're not omniscient. We're human, we're finite, our knowledge has limits. We don't have the power to sway the future. We imagine we have a measure of control over things like time, finances, and health. But it's an illusion. Life is far more fragile.

Where I live, the mere threat of snow becomes big news. We're sucked into nonstop news coverage where every five minutes they cut to the guy at the airport for an update. Of course he has to play along, unable to say the obvious: "No different than five minutes ago when you asked me. And why do we always take readings at the airport anyway? Nobody lives here." He sticks with the routine, though the snow hasn't started yet. And people are freaking out. One pastor I know whose church rents their facility told me the landlord shut them down Wednesday over a forecast of snow on Sunday. A forecast! Where will all this lead? Will they eventually close the city from December to April?

I'm joking. Actually, I'm not. I think we often crave risk-free living. But if you eliminate risks, you obliterate ambition.

When God "constrains" us by his Spirit to do something, he doesn't fill in all the blanks. We must trust him, just like Paul trusted him. Risk exists because we can't control events and we don't know what's going to happen. In other words, when we don't know the future, we find out whom we really trust.

We're called not to control the future, but to trust God for it.

Do you feel called in a direction but are uncertain about what will happen? God's design in that is to drive you to dependence upon him. Have you noticed how your desperation for God increases with the uncertainty in your life? The new job, the new child, that new ministry—all of a sudden we're desperate for God. We're starved, needy, ravished by a hunger to hear. God delights to put us in this position because it postures us to depend on him and to exercise faith toward him. It's part of how he rescues us from misplaced security.

Risk always leads us to experience God in a deeper way. This is by design. Risk rescues us from misplaced security by anchoring us in the eternal.

Claim Two: Prepare for Difficulty

Here's the second claim: prepare for difficulty, because ambition also rescues us from distracting comforts.

In the account of Paul's words at Miletus to the Ephesian elders, Acts 20:22–23 adds a curious twist:

> And now, behold, I am going to Jerusalem, constrained by the Spirit, not knowing what will happen to me there, *except that the Holy Spirit testifies to me in every city that imprisonment and afflictions await me.*

Now it's getting dicey. God doesn't tell Paul everything about the future, but he does let him in on this little secret: imprisonment and afflictions await him.

If I were Paul, I'd appeal to renegotiate this deal. "Lord, can we do this one of two ways? Either give me the whole picture of what's coming, or don't tell me anything. But if you're going to grant me just a peek, does it have to be about prison and pain?"

Paul knew that indulging his ambition for the gospel would bring danger and difficulties. But he was called to go forward anyway. He had a sense for the ending; he just didn't know how it would happen. Remember on *Star Trek* when the no-name crew members would beam down with the regular crew? You knew what that was all about. They were alien bait, and this episode was about to get interesting. You had a sense for the ending; you just didn't know the particulars. That was Paul.

Why does God want us to know that difficulty will accompany the pursuit of our ambitions?

This raises a question: Why? Why does God tell Paul there's difficulty up ahead? Why does God want us to know that difficulty will accompany the pursuit of our ambitions?

Because our natural tendency is to seek the least challenging way. Are you like me? I often want to eliminate risk, eradicate cost, and keep difficulties at bay. That was my problem in the cave with my son. And it's my problem anytime the gospel mission threatens my comfort.

But the Christian life calls us to pick up the cross, not a recliner. God promises that all who follow Christ will meet trial and tribulation (John 16:33; James 1:2–3). All that comes with the journey. In Acts 20:23, Paul doesn't say, "I only know that hotels and Jacuzzis await me." I wish. Instead he says, "I only know that imprisonment and afflictions await me."

If you want to glorify God through godly ambition, prepare for difficulties. God has a unique design in them. Sometimes they're life preservers. Difficulties strip down and violate our comforts, keeping us rooted in what really matters. Godly ambition rescues us from the distraction of trying to follow Christ and seek comfort at the same time.

One of the ways our great prosperity in the West fails to serve Christians is that it makes comfort more achievable. We have comfort food, Select Comfort beds, even Comfort Inns. Type "comfort" into a search engine and you'll get the Comfort House, an entire store that styles itself as "The Source for Products That Make Your Life Easier." Only in America.

But not all Americans are distracted by comfort. Constrained by the Spirit, Bob and Joanne pursued their godly ambition. They moved forward, knowing that difficulties would come.

Their life is never dull. "We live in a strange land because of Christopher's medical complexities," Joanne explained. "He is stable and fragile at the same time. The threat of rejection to the transplanted organs always looms in the shadows. There are always difficulties, and we could easily become discouraged. But God continually pours out grace and faith for the journey."

How can a family face that kind of difficulty—even taking on more challenges with the addition of each new foster child—with such hope? Only with godly ambition.

Some time ago, I traveled with some other pastors to conduct two conferences for leaders in Africa. One conference was hosted by an African leader who was trained in a United States seminary. While here, his younger kids became entirely oriented to Western culture. They spent nearly five years enjoying things most Americans take for granted—good health care, take-out pizza, the NBA. As his graduation neared, something unexpected happened. He began to wrestle with questions about whether he should go back. Why should he risk transplanting his family back to the poverty and problems of his country when by staying they could have a good income, fast food, dental care, and five-dollar cups of coffee?

His answer echoes Paul's response in Acts 20:24: "I do not account my life of any value nor as precious to myself, if only I may finish my course and the ministry that I received from the Lord Jesus, to testify to the gospel of the grace of God." My African friend made an uncomfortable choice: to pursue his ambition to preach the gospel in his native country.

I think we as Westerners could use a big dose of faith that comes from the risk of dangerous gospel assignments. But in looking for the big risk, we can also overlook the little risks, and the faith that comes from accepting them. Sometimes the ministry we walk right past each Sunday or the neighbors we wave to at a distance are the very risks where gospel ambition lays claim to us.

What is the Spirit-constrained ambition that God wants us to indulge for his glory right where we are?

When Paul says, "I am going to Jerusalem, not knowing what will happen," he's speaking within his role and responsibility. The questions we must ask are, What's our Jerusalem? What is the Spirit-constrained ambition that God wants us to indulge for his glory right where we are?

Following his message at the 2008 Together for the Gospel Conference, John Piper was asked how people can live sacrificially for the gospel when they're not presently facing trial or aren't sensing a call to relocate to a place where risk is a way of life. Piper had this to say:

> Find the hard stuff, get satisfied in Jesus, find him sufficiently motivating, and enjoy the fellowship of his sufferings. Have you ever heard anybody say, "While walking on the primrose path of sunshine I discovered the deepest and most lasting fellowship with Jesus"?

Never. . . .

Always and without exception—and I have never heard anybody gainsay this—human beings say, "I met him most, I went deepest with him, I enjoyed him, I saw more of him on my dark road, on my hard road." And so why would we not embrace commanded hard roads like evangelism or anything that will stress you?[2]

That's in-your-face biblical logic for us all. Nothing mortifies the craving for comfort more quickly than embracing a hard road.

And some of us are there right now. We're compelled by God with an ambition, we've sought counsel, and now we must move forward. We must take a step.

Some of us may *need* to be there right now. We're too comfortable. We haven't taken a risk since Reagan left the White House. We can't pursue ambition because we fear risk, yet we're underchallenged, under-ambitious. We're on the Primrose Path of Sunshine, and we're bored beyond belief.

Let me ask you: what Spirit-constrained risk is God calling you to take?

Maybe it's finally getting fully involved in that church you've been visiting for months. Maybe it's going from two incomes to one so you can parent your kids in a more hands-on way. Maybe it's not waiting for the church to start an outreach ministry and just reaching out yourself. Maybe it's coming out of retirement and into the strategic use of your time and resources to serve others.

Godly ambition doesn't demand to know the future, protect our comforts, or seek to eliminate risk. It steps forward in faith. Ambition drives onward knowing that God is glorified in us when the gospel goes forth through our sacrifices.

God loves us too much to allow us to squander another moment in the great twilight of ambivalence. The only risk-free life is in the next world. To have godly ambition, we must accept risk.

Claim Three: Value the Gospel above All

The Fannon family is quite a sight. When moving together, they're a traveling advertisement for the joys and challenges of godly ambition. At one time, between all their children, the entourage included wheelchairs, IV poles, ventilators, oxygen tanks, and food pumps. With all the children, plus all the equipment, they need multiple cars and multiple drivers to travel as a family. The mere burden of traveling often confines the family to their home—it's just easier.

Why on earth would they do this—accept a child requiring special medical training and round-the-clock care? Christopher didn't just alter their daily routine; he obliterated it. Why would the Fannons willingly embrace these risks?

"It's the gospel," says Joanne, "It drives everything! The gospel is about God loving the unlovely through Christ—and calling us to do the same. It's reaching those who can't help themselves. Parenting kids who no one else can is our way of showing God's love to them."

The Fannons made a decision years ago that governs their life each day. They would cherish the gospel above all. "We will value the gospel above all else, and trust God with the rest," says Joanne. "We've had kids suffer and some die; when it costs so much to believe the gospel every day, that's when it's made most valuable."

Paul took different risks, but he was after the same prize. Listen again to what he said: "I do not account my life of any value nor as precious to myself," he said, "if only I may finish my course . . . to testify to the gospel of the grace of God."

Gospel ambitions can be audacious because they stake out some unorthodox assumptions. Paul is saying, "Even though I have gifts and responsibilities, I'm not too strategic or important to be uprooted for the sake of the gospel." As he spoke to the Ephesian elders, he made it clear that he prized the gospel above his reputation. That's why he didn't shrink back from declaring "the whole counsel of God" (Acts 20:27).

Paul also talks about how he prizes the gospel even more than friendships. What makes this especially poignant is that it obviously wasn't easy for him. Paul was deeply relational. He wasn't just circulating through the body of Christ unaccountable, unattached. The Ephesian elders were his buddies, his mates. He'd lived with them and served them with tears. As Paul's ship sails away, you can imagine the elders saying, "The gospel just took the best we've got." That's pretty audacious. But God understands. He sent out his best as well, in the person of Jesus Christ.

Our comforts or income level are not too important to be sacrificed for the gospel.

Paul's ambition was not randomly pointed at many goals, all equally important. Nope, Paul valued the gospel above all things. Even Paul's life wasn't more precious than that. For us to follow his example, it might mean deciding, "I'm not too important to exercise ambition for the gospel" or "My comforts or income level are not too important to be sacrificed for the gospel."

Twelve years after Christopher Fannon came home, he's still alive. He brings joy to Bob and Joanne and to all who come in contact with their family. Other kids have also come into the Fannon home—a total of eleven, to be exact. They're a poignant parable of God's great love for us. Every day the Fannons live out gospel ambitions as they pour out faith and love kids in desperate need of adoption and care.

Their world was no "roll of the dice." No, they accepted risks built upon the most certain of all foundations. Risks for the sake of the risk-worthy gospel of Jesus Christ. Risks that expressed their faith in the One who called them. Risks that evidenced their practice of "pure and undefiled . . . religion" (James 1:27).

God made the Fannons with hearts for this type of care and this type of ministry. He stirred an ambition to provide a family for those in greatest need. "I think God gave us the faith to seek out the sickest of the sick, to bring them home to live the remainder of their lives with our family," Joanne says. "To give them the gift of hope through Jesus Christ and to pour out the love that has been poured out upon our hearts and home."

One Final Call

Is the fear of risk still looming large in your mind? Good. Risk is nothing to be ignored. It must be accounted for and acknowledged.

But while you spend some time studying the reality of all the risks staring your ambition square in the eyes, don't lose sight of the most important thing.

Risk for risk's sake is reckless. God isn't calling you to that. But he's calling you to great risk *for the gospel.*

So strive for a faith where the gospel looms largest in your vision. Strive for a joy that finds its greatest fulfillment in the expansion of the gospel.

We ought to honor the faith of the Fannons. We ought to deeply respect Paul's sacrifice and trust. But we're not supposed to admire from the sidelines. Let your ambition get you off the bench and into the game. Admire these heroes by running alongside them. Stare risk in the face, and declare that you won't be owned by your fears. You serve a great God who purchased you with his blood. He, not your fears, will determine your steps. He holds the future, and he's called you to run hard after it.

So what do you do now? What's one practical step you can take to be equipped to share the gospel? What's one step you can take to actually share the gospel?

I was at a wedding the other day, talking with one of the guests, and was making an effort to share the gospel with him. I was glad for the opportunity, but I felt unprepared. I realized I need to get a refresher on how to effectively share Christ. Do you?

Maybe you dream of pastoral ministry, and reading this book stirs something in you. Maybe you long to carry the gospel to people who need it by starting new churches. Have you talked to your pastor? Are you serving in the church you're already attending? Are you reading good theology and immersing yourself in the Scriptures?

Parents, is God calling you to a risky love for your children? Maybe your ambition right now is to cultivate the kind of love that shows kindness and mercy even when we want to punish, the love that puts off self-righteousness and puts on gentleness. Are you ambitious that your children see the gospel through you?

From time to time opportunities for extraordinary risk come to our lives. Are you prepared to see those opportunities and respond to them with godly ambition? But don't wait for the extraordinary—the Christian life is inherently risky every day, if we care to take it seriously. It will risk our comfort, our agendas, our downtime, our nest eggs, and our reputations, in big ways and small.

Whatever that risk is, are you resolved to pursue Christ? Do you prize the glorious truth of his righteous life, his death in our place, and his resurrection and return? Are you determined to, like Christ, pursue *downward* mobility?

God stokes the fire of ambition in the souls of men and women. He fans the flame and calls us to expect a big God to do great things. Ambition requires risk; it's the cost of progress and proclamation. And in risk the gospel of Jesus Christ marches forward unexpectedly, unceasingly, unstoppable. Whether it's going to Jerusalem, adopting special-needs children, or crossing the street to talk with a neighbor, we all get to play a part.

It's a paradox: ambition needs to be rescued from the "me" trap, but God turns the tables and uses holy ambition to rescue *us*. He delivers us from flimsy security and harmful comforts. He sets us free to live for his kingdom.

Oh, and by the way, I just got word from the Fannons today. Risk knocked on their door this week in the form of a baby girl, her tiny body devastated by chemotherapy. Their response? You guessed it, they couldn't be more excited. They're already busy pursuing the adoption, lining up the surgeries, and praying for miracles. They live largely unaware that their passion for adopting babies with chronic health problems is, in itself, a miracle.

Only with God is this possible. Only with God.

11

Ambition Paid Forward

THE MISSION MARCHES ON WHEN AMBITION LOOKS AHEAD

"Lead the way!"

The words were directed at my oldest son as he stood saluting the combat-decorated master sergeant. It was the pivotal moment of the commissioning ceremony when Army cadets officially receive the rank of second lieutenant.

The master sergeant had marched forward in parade precision and was stopping sharply only inches from each cadet. He would snap a salute, then address them for the first time as officers. Locking eyes with each cadet, he issued his final order to them: "Lead the way!"

The ceremonial response from each infantry cadet was, "Follow me!"

It was all part of a solemn Army ritual to signify that this next generation of leaders was receiving a real mantle of responsibility.

The weight of tradition was palpable as each young cadet stood waiting for this exchange with the master sergeant. Each was only one salute away from receiving rank. Each had waited four years to hear, "Lead the way."

I'd never been to a commissioning ceremony before, unless you count the day I hit tenderfoot during my summer of scouting. This was way more serious. If you're like me and don't know military ranks, the master sergeant is one of the highest enlisted rankings. This guy standing in front of my son was—well, if you're ever in a fight, you want him on your side. In fact, you may not need anybody else. This career soldier had served in Special Forces and had traveled to almost every country in the world. He was a sniper master and an airborne and air assault instructor certified and allowed to wear combat boots with his dress blues. If all of that means little to you, just know that in the Army world it's just short of a PhD. For me, it meant I would try in no way to tick him off.

The master sergeant had been the instructor responsible for training the cadets over the last three years. He met them at 5 AM every morning, drilled them, taught them, evaluated them, and screamed creative obscenities at them. He was the point man, meaning the Army had given him a personal mandate to deliver the cadets to the commissioning ceremony ready to take charge.

But here's the irony: the very second after their commissioning, each of these young second lieutenants would outrank this battle-hardened master sergeant. This meant, among other things, that they could actually issue him an order. It wasn't recommended, but it was technically possible.

But at the moment of that long-awaited salute, the leader became the follower. It was the older serving the younger, the experienced making a way for the next generation. A transfer had taken place.

The Army honors this tradition because they understand something very important: ambition must stretch to the next generation. True success means not just building something, but passing it on to a younger generation. I'm talking about turning over real responsibility, locking eyes, snapping a proverbial salute, and saying, "Lead the way."

Always Looking Ahead

Imagine an ambition that grows stronger as you get older. One so clear and indomitable it reaches into the next generation.

Roger and Dottie Small were married September 21, 1958. One year after their wedding day, they welcomed their first daughter into their family. Soon following were two more girls.

The next several years were filled with kid stuff—school, sports, trips to the doctor, many memories, family vacations, and many hours building into their local church. The Smalls built a family life that was based in the church.

Fast-forward many years. All the girls have married godly men and moved on to start their own families. For most, that would signal the opportunity for their parents to slow down and relax.

But not Roger and Dottie. Recently I sat with one of their sons-in-law, Warren Boettcher. From his front-row seat Warren said, "Roger and Dottie view themselves as existing for the next generation."

The Smalls live an extraordinary life. Twenty-five years after their youngest daughter moved out, they still have a laundry list of activities—hosting evangelistic outreach, worship band practice, small groups, counseling sessions, classes. The list goes on. But it's not about their activity. It's about why they do it. It's about their ambition for the next generation.

"Roger and Dottie," Warren said, "have a humility that positions them not as experts but as learners. Sometimes older saints have a this-is-how-we-did-it mentality. But not Roger and Dottie. They don't tell the next generation how to live. They find out what the next generation is doing and ask how they can help. Their lives are oriented to serve."

This really provokes me. But there's more. When most people their age were downsizing, Roger and Dottie were building a four-bedroom house with nine-foot ceilings in the basement. Why? Because they anticipated the day when the basement would need to be an apartment for a family member, a young couple, a single mom. Recently Roger and Dottie moved into one of the bedrooms and converted the dining room to their living room. They occupy two rooms in their house so that their daughter and son-in-law and their children can use the rest of the house.

"Because Roger and Dottie built their house for this very reason, they don't view living in two rooms of their own house as a sacrifice," said Warren. "There is just no retirement mentality in them."

The Smalls' ambition for the next generation—and for the one after that—should inspire us. They've redefined the golden years according to a higher call. Every purchase they make, every investment, every decision is with an eye to how it will serve the next generation and be used for the future.

If you ask the Smalls' children, grandchildren, and great-grandchildren, they'll tell you that gratitude and humility mark Roger and Dottie's lives. "Roger and Dottie," Warren said, "see life through multiple generations."

Is that the way you see life?

We've covered a lot of ground in this book. Perhaps you feel, as I do, that we've traveled to some unusual places together. We've heard ambition's cry for help. We've seen that godly ambition must be rescued from the popular assumption that it's toxic. We've seen how the right kind of dreams lead us to long for the things God has called us to and to pursue them with passion that burns deep and long. Our ambitions for God must follow God's ambitions for us.

Before we close, I want you to dream with me. What would it be like to have ambition that reaches beyond ourselves and toward the generations that come after us? An ambition that identifies, trains, and then releases others and tells them, "Lead the way!"

The Story of My Salute

It's that question that led me to an unlikely place on October 12, 2008.

On that Sunday morning, I stood on a stage in front of the church I'd been privileged to lead for nineteen years, performing my last act as their senior pastor. I was handing off my role as senior pastor to a twenty-eight-year-old guy named Jared Mellinger.

But this transfer had an unusual twist to it, captured in the final ordination vow:

> Do you promise to begin praying for your ultimate replacement in ministry, with the hope of one day identifying, training, and transferring your responsibilities to him, so that this church may continue to grow and mature in future generations, for the glory and honor of God?

"I do," came the response.

The transfer was complete. Covenant Fellowship Church, a twenty-five-year-old congregation in the Philadelphia area, had a new senior pastor (a very gifted one, I might add). Although Jared was barely navigating a tricycle when the church was planted, he'd just officially accepted his role to lead the congregation. And he did so with the unusual provision that he, too, would begin immediately planning to one day transfer his role to a qualified younger man.

Jared hadn't even preached his first sermon in this new role, yet he was already thinking about his replacement. He was promising to be ambitious for a generation yet unborn. And the pastoral team and people of Covenant Fellowship Church were willing to say, "Lead the way!"

Several paths of ambition converged on that Sunday morning, all part of the story of what can happen when an entire church has a dream to transfer the gospel to the next generation.

> The only thing remarkable about this story is
> the grace and mercy of God in some
> pretty ordinary people.

Let me say from the outset that the only thing remarkable about this story is the grace and mercy of God in some pretty ordinary people, including myself. It's a snapshot of what happens when God rescues ambition for his glory. He takes our ambition for the gospel and turns it toward the future. Gospel-centered becomes gospel-transferring.

You may be saying, "Oh great, Dave, but how does this apply to *me* in my job, my school, my world?" Please don't get caught up in the particulars of this story. By looking past the surface, you'll observe something that captures the heart of this book. When godly ambition flourishes in our lives, powerful things begin to happen. God's sovereign purposes unfold through the agency of human initiative, and God alone receives the glory. No one else could bring together the four paths of ambition like he has in this story. Only God. And to stand where these paths converge is, in my view, to stand on holy ground.

Path One: Ambition Released

After twenty-five years, Bill Patton still loves his church. That's a good thing, since he started it.

Bill was in the congregation on that Sunday in October 2008 when Jared became senior pastor. Back in 1984, he'd led the team of families and singles who started this church. Bill came to the

Philadelphia suburbs with a passion to preach the gospel, build a church, and see young men trained as leaders.

Bill saw in me the potential gifts to preach and pastor. So shortly after moving to Philadelphia at age twenty-six to be part of this church plant, I joined the church staff as a greenhorn and began experiencing the thrill of caring for God's people. The church was planning to send me out within two years to start another church in Pittsburgh, my hometown—home of the Steelers!

But things didn't go as any of us planned. Without warning some things occurred in Bill's family that made it clear he needed to step out of his role as senior pastor. The natural decision was to turn the church over to the other founding pastor, which is exactly what happened. But within a few months this man humbly concluded that he didn't have the gifts to be senior pastor.

So the role fell to the last man available, the least experienced guy who already had one foot out the door. Yep, me.

Before I go further, I want to pause and direct your attention to some particulars on my friend Bill. In deciding to step down as senior pastor, he hadn't been involved in immorality or financial misconduct. The issue was the effect Bill's significant responsibility for the leadership of the church was having on his primary responsibility to lead his home. It had become clear to Bill and others around him that the pastoral role Bill needed to play in his home required him to step out of the pastoral leadership of the church.

Bill is a very gifted man, gifted to preach and lead. He comes from a Christian family and had a lifelong desire to serve God in pastoral ministry. Bill loved being the senior pastor. He loved preaching and enjoyed the adventure of leading a growing church. Under his leadership the church had gathered several hundred people quickly and was continuing to grow. His ambition was to spend his life leading a church.

But now he realized he needed to step away from that. God was calling him to let go of his aspirations and to walk the less traveled path of ambition released.

So here's the scene: a gifted Christian leader, who founds and leads a fruitful ministry, faces a decision that will set the course for his own future and the future of his church. He can claim that the issues he's dealing with aren't that big of a deal. He can find loopholes, exegetical back doors for escape from the biblical qualifications for eldership. The church is young, and there aren't any other great leaders waiting in the wings. Wouldn't it be best to just stay on the present course and work things out as well as possible? Lesser men have reasoned this way. There's a kind of selfish ambition that seeks to legitimize a campaign to hold on to what you have at any cost.

Or he could simply redefine his understanding of Scripture, or even his sense of call. You know, find a different type of ministry where his family's health wasn't an impediment to his giftings. It would have been easy to do what is growing more common—simply stand up and speak of being mystically called to a new venture for God, wishing the church all the best for the future as you turn your back and walk out the door. Thomas Watson observed, "Selfish ambition is the mother of all schisms."[1] The wrong kind of ambition can push you to change your convictions to fit your opportunities.

Bill had his options and his temptations, but God gave him clarity on something important. Sometimes honoring God means taking your ambition to the altar. As Abraham did with Isaac, and as Hannah did with her desire for a child, you can take what you believe God has given you and offer it back to him.

So Bill showed himself to be a man whose true passion was a love for Christ and his church. He stood courageously before the people who had come together under his leadership, and he turned the church over to others.

But it didn't stop there. He publicly committed himself to be an active and enthusiastic member of the church he'd founded—to support this church through the transition and to serve them long into the future. He also dedicated himself to leading his family with gospel humility.

Where does a man gain that kind of courage and fortitude when he must let go of his ambitions? You guessed it: the gospel. Listen to the words of this man who paid a price to live what he believes:

> The gospel answers my questions of identity. It tells me I am God's
> bondservant, his child, a worshiper, and a functioning member of

his church. My identity as a pastor was always a secondary identity. I have not lost my main identity.

The gospel answers my questions about purpose. The gospel opened my eyes to the glory of God in Christ. I responded to the call to ministry in order to glorify God. Being a pastor was never, rightly, my chief end. I do not presently have opportunity to serve as a pastor, but I do have daily opportunities to fulfill my main purpose in life. Asking the question, "How do I glorify God *now?*" wonderfully liberates me.

The gospel also points the way to my ongoing happiness. My main joy is in God and in the salvation Jesus wrought for me on the cross. Above all else, I'm grateful to be a Christian—to be saved—to know the joy of sins forgiven and conscience cleansed. The joy of ministry could never legitimately be the foundation of my happiness. It is a secondary, derivative joy.

So, God has taught me to . . .

—think of myself in terms of my main identity.

—busy myself with my main purpose.

—delight myself in my main joy.

Over the years, Bill's desire to return to pastoral ministry hasn't died. And perhaps one day this ambition will be realized. But Bill's ambitions, even noble ones, don't rule him. His convictions rule his ambitions. He believes that serving the church matters more than securing a position in ministry, that passing the gospel to our children is more important than having our dream job, and that God's glory is infinitely more important than personal fulfillment.

To this day, Bill is a passionately committed member of Covenant Fellowship Church. Our church is stronger because he's in it. And Bill's hard work in pastoring his family is bearing good fruit and producing an ongoing testimony in its own right. Bill's son Chris planted a growing church in nearby Delaware. Wow, that's some serious fruit.

Bill has taught us all that our greatest impact might be in the way we live outside the spotlight—how we exalt grace, apply the gospel, and pursue true biblical ambition. Bill wasn't living for the moment. Turning over what he founded to another was more important than protecting his position or safeguarding his name. He saw he needed to release his ambition to preserve the future. The gospel was more important than Bill's dreams.

Bill's ambition had been rescued.

Path Two: Ambition Sanctified

As I prepared to turn leadership of Covenant Fellowship Church over to Jared, more than one person asked me why I was doing this.

I could understand the question. I wasn't hitting retirement age—yet. Sure, I was taking on a new role in Sovereign Grace Ministries, the group my church is part of, but I wasn't trying to get kicked up to corporate. I loved pastoral ministry, and I loved my church, which was large and growing. With a couple of executive pastors, a pastoral team of over a dozen men, and a thriving evangelistic program, there were always new people and new initiatives to make ministry a continuing adventure and ceaseless source of joy.

Being senior pastor of a large suburban church may not seem like a big deal to you. But I have a habit of chasing my own glory, and this was a position I once would have fought to keep. That's why I want you to hear a bit of my story. It's the story of how God set me on the path of ambition sanctified.

Nineteen years ago, I was a wet-behind-the-ears pastor with a degree in criminology whose only area of expertise was seventies pop music. Frankly, folks probably should have headed for the exits when I became the senior pastor. I was ambitious to lead but had no idea what that really meant. All I knew was that I should run hard in the direction God called me. But running hard was all I knew. Running for God's glory had yet to be learned.

Ever since my conversion, I've felt a strong impulse to do something important for God, to develop my gifts, to just throw myself into whatever it was God was doing. Even as an unbeliever I was wired for initiative—a quality my friends loved, but among their parents it won me the award for Most Likely to Create Problems for Our Kids. I distinctly remember that certain drives developed as I grew in Christ. I wanted to live with intention, to plot a course, to advocate ideas, to persuade people. Basically, I wanted to lead. I had a consuming ambition for my life to count. Oh, and did I mention that I love to work?

Maybe you can relate to that ("Hey, he's like me"). Or maybe this personality is less appealing to you ("Hey, he's, like, weird"). The point is that my quarter century of pastoring isn't about ambition fulfilled but about ambition transformed. To be more biblically precise, it's about ambition sanctified.

For me, ambition is a double-edged sword. For years all I saw was the shiny side of the blade. It took God's carefully designed discipline to begin opening my eyes to the rusty underside of selfish ambition.

In his mercy God allowed me to lead a wonderful church—and in the process he used the circumstances of that position to transform my motive for serving as I struggled with selfish ambition.

Early in my preaching career if I told a story about myself, I often looked good. Real good. Too good. I guess I figured, "Hey, as long as I have the microphone, why not polish my reputation a bit?"

It happened in private as well. Conversations became a Dave-fest. The subtle sprinkling of data was designed to raise my stock in the mental market of others. It wasn't always conscious, but it happened nonetheless.

When Kimm and my friends began pointing out this tendency, I was appalled at my naked grab for glory. It was ugly. But to rescue ambition, God first rescues us from ugly. That's the way it worked for me.

Now I actually *enjoy* telling people about my failures and frailties. Sure, it's humbling. But it's also far more accurate. I figure everyone knows I'm a sinner anyway, so why leave them speculating on how I sin? I might as well tell them. Even if they can't relate to my sin, they can identify with me as a sinner.

Another example: There was a day when, if our family of churches was holding a conference, I was usually asked to speak. By the grace of God, other gifted men came along, and the pool of potential speakers deepened. This meant I wasn't as "needed."

"So, Dave," you ask, "did you thank God that God's people were being served by gifted men who might serve more effectively than you?"

Heck no. I began to feel displaced. I grew discontented, and I complained in my heart. I slid toward the "disorder and vile practices" of James 3:16. While outwardly I showed support, inwardly my soul began to spiral into the chaos of selfish ambition.

Maybe you know what I'm talking about. We become discouraged because we're not doing what we think we're called and gifted to do or what we used to find fulfillment in. Maybe someone moves ahead of us on the track of our vision. Or maybe we're just diverted to another track that seems to offer less fulfillment for our dreams. So we question God—his goodness, his wisdom, his power, his love. We turn from God to self. Remember *incurvatus in se*—the heart's penchant for curving in on itself. And when self is the reference point for ambition, nothing good comes from it.

God loves us too much to allow us to settle for self.

But God loves us too much to allow us to settle for self. That was my story.

I began to realize God ordained that experience not to simply reveal I had ambition but to show me that my ambition was corrupted by the "love of distinction" about which Timothy Dwight warned the Princeton graduates. In my selfish ambition I want to be big. I didn't need to be the biggest fish in the ocean, but I did need to be a big fish in my little pond. Which is really the same thing when you think about it. I also needed everyone, including other big fish, to look at me and say, "Now that's a *big fish*—and a handsome and smart one as well." It took me a while to realize that my big, bloated fish-self was starting to stink.

Yep, in my attempts to be great, I can get pretty small.

Can you relate? Maybe that's why you've gotten this far in this book. Maybe it's happening to you right now. The boss redefined your role, the coach changed your position, your husband redirected today's to-do list. Those moments are a great index for measuring desires. It's the routine of life, where roles and agendas are changed without our approval, that reveals ambition for self.

But here's what God was teaching me in the process. And this is truly amazing. Those impulses for attaining and preserving my position are no longer what define me. That doesn't mean I'm never tempted to make much of myself. I certainly am. But by the grace of

God I've learned to discern my ambitions before I let them determine my path.

On the day I stood before the church announcing our belief that Jared should replace me, there was an indescribable joy in my heart. God had done a sanctifying work in me. He replaced my selfish ambitions with godly ones. Of course, this book is not a testimony to the finished work of God in my life. Believe me, there's still a ways to go when it comes to sanctifying my ambitions. But God has taken a man of high ambition and molded him into a man who's learning to pursue godly ambitions more and more.

One of the ways God transformed my ambition was to change its focus. In his kindness he shifted my dreams away from myself and toward the generation that would follow mine. I began to realize that godly ambition means I think about what happens after I'm gone. It means we carry a passion to transfer an understanding of the gospel to our children, and to their children, and to theirs. Ambition began to grow in me for what Psalm 78:4 describes: "We will not hide them from their children, but tell to the coming generation the glorious deeds of the LORD."

To apply this work in my heart to real life, I committed myself to teaching the church that ours was not a one-generation work. To be truly and biblically ambitious, our dreams need to reach into the next generation. This included reminding them that I would one day be replaced as pastor, and when that day came, it would be a joyful occasion. I wanted to remind them—and myself—that another generation was emerging. A biblical definition of success means we transfer the work to them, positioning them to run stronger and farther, while we cheer them on. Publicly I was now on the timer. And I now had an accountability group of a thousand or so people with a vested interest in how I walked this out.

Needless to say, I began to pray and look aggressively for my replacement. One of the things that has made a great difference for a hard-driving man like me is the example of some of my friends. Their selflessness is a daily challenge to my own selfishness. I have a friend named Mark whose response to any service opportunity is something like, "I'll be happy to serve for as long as I'm needed." I love that response because it's laced with gospel humility. It says, "I won't hold you hostage to keeping me in a role when it's time to move on." I've seen that in others, like C. J. Mahaney, who was among the first in our family of churches to turn over the reins of leadership to the younger generation. Men like this helped shape my perspective on what gospel-centered ambition really is.

As I stood on the stage with Jared on that Sunday morning of the actual transfer, there was no doubt in my mind: only God could have rescued my ambition by sanctifying it.

Path Three: Ambition Refined

Over time, this ambition for something beyond ourselves and our generation has soaked into the pastoral culture of our church. As our team looked to the future, we wanted our children to understand, celebrate, and proclaim the gospel even more than we had. But we saw that this would require us to conform our personal ambitions to what was best for the church. This meant the church couldn't be a career in the traditional sense. Ministry was a call to serve. It also meant the whole concept of "my ministry" would need to be reexamined in light of Scripture.

When the church breathes the air of a consumer culture, it rarely gets enough oxygen to survive. Godly motives for true service gasp for breath while a baser motivation—"ministry as personal fulfillment"—thrives. *My* ministry" becomes a virus that sucks the health and life from a local church.

The church shouldn't merely accommodate
our ministry; it should help define it
according to the present needs of the church.

Now don't get me wrong; we want to see people identify their gifts and use them in the church. The problem is when the church becomes a stage, and our gifts are the featured performers. This moves way beyond encouraging ambition to empowering selfish ambition.

The church shouldn't merely accommodate our ministry; it

should help define it according to the present needs of the church. And this is true for everyone—not just the full-time pastors. This means if you have a burden for adult education but the church needs someone to teach kids, then grab the milk and cookies and get your lessons ready. Service comes before gifts. It reveals and refines them.

So as a team of pastors, we made some specific affirmations. I don't remember where the idea came from. It may have been that we saw the need to summarize a collection of values the pastoral team accumulated over the years as we walked the path of ambition refined. It may have been that our pastoral team was changing over time, and we wanted to make sure all of us—both seasoned vets and the new blood—were aligned in our vision for our roles in the church. It certainly came from a realization that we need something more than good intentions to live out the convictions we were expressing.

So during one fall retreat, convened specifically for our mutual encouragement and care, we formally affirmed to each other a number of values. Here's what each member of our pastoral team committed himself to individually:

> I affirm the value of *devotion* by remembering that my identity is in Christ, not in my ministry, position, calling, or the approval of man. My greatest joy and fulfillment is to live as his servant for the glory of his name.
>
> I affirm the value of *humility* by encouraging the men around me to help me assess my strengths and weaknesses of both character and gifting, and working with them to position me for the best benefit of the church and the mission of the gospel.
>
> I affirm the value of *honesty* by committing to sharing my opinions in a way that to the best of my understanding is humble and constructive—and in the same manner to also share any struggles I have with the team, its members, or its decisions.
>
> I affirm the value of *integrity* by taking responsibility to open my life and my family to evaluation and care.
>
> I affirm the value of *accountability* by committing to lay my life before the team in light of the biblical qualifications for ministry. I recognize and affirm that the responsibility of evaluating my qualifications is the responsibility of the church and its leaders.

I affirm the value of *faithfulness* by looking for, praying for, and—where possible—training and promoting my ultimate replacement in ministry so the church may continue to grow and mature into future generations.

I affirm the value of *unity* by acknowledging that I will seek to do all I can to represent the values of team ministry in the local church while I'm serving in vocational ministry, and to continue doing so if and when that service ever ends.

Likewise, together as a team we committed ourselves specifically "to seek God together for the best positioning of each man, to bring encouragement where we see God's grace in his life and ministry, to bring loving observations and correction where there may be weakness or error, and to seek God-exalting goals for his future growth as a pastor, husband, and father."

We also felt the need, individually, to make some serious acknowledgments in connection with these values. For example, regarding *humility*:

I acknowledge that one of the temptations of ministry that increases with time is the desire for personal fulfillment—a sense that the longer I'm in ministry, the more my personal sense of gifts and vision should form the contours of my ministry. In fact, the longer I'm in ministry, the more I need others' help to keep me from settling into what could be comfortable employment rather than sacrificial service for Christ and his church. . . .

And concerning *honesty*:

I acknowledge the temptation to want either to withhold my perspective to avoid evaluation of my motives, or to express my opinions as if they're ideas disconnected from desires of my heart. . . .

And regarding *faithfulness*:

I acknowledge the temptation to fear the ultimate transition out of ministry and seek to protect my position on the team. I will battle this fear and the striving and ambition that accompany it by embracing evaluation of my gifts and call as an ongoing necessity. . . .

I'll never forget that retreat. Looking around the room and considering the quality of men I've been joined to—some for more than twenty years—humbles me even now. Any number of these guys could lead their own church. I can't believe God gave me the privilege of leading them for close to twenty years. And boy, are they diverse. One pastor was an NBC producer before entering pastoral ministry. Another was a corporate executive. Another worked in politics. Another loves photography and writing and can field dress a deer that he just killed with his bow. I've often thought our unity should be offered as a proof that there's a God.

We all get along great. But these affirmations don't come into play when everybody is reading off the same page. They're meant to govern our actions and words in times where the next thing we do will either build up or tear down the work God is doing in our church. Affirmations like these are not testimonies to our strength but testimonies to our weaknesses—and to the corrupting power of selfish ambition if it ever gets a foothold in our pastoral team.

Maybe these kinds of affirmations can serve you in your church or business or home. What we desire to pass on to the future must be affirmed and preserved in the present. That's the secret to refined ambition.

Path Four: Ambition Embodied

The desire of a few to transfer the gospel will never truly accomplish the goal. Godly ambition must be embodied by a people willing to collectively say, "Lead the way."

I'll never forget the morning we told the church that we thought God was calling Jared to replace me as the new senior pastor. Our church family was neither neutral nor silent. They erupted in applause. There was a standing ovation that lasted for a few minutes.

I love my church, but never more than in that moment. And from that moment Covenant Fellowship Church committed to participate in the process. They prayed for Jared, helped evaluate him as a leader, affirmed his calling to lead the church, then wholeheartedly committed to follow this young man as their next senior pastor. But this is just one example in a church that for more than two decades has nurtured an ambition to pass the gospel of Christ to the next generation.

Another example is Marty, a guy who never really "felt called" to children's ministry but persevered in service there because he was needed. He realized we didn't have a good curriculum to train the next generation in gospel truth. So he wrote some—and in the process discovered a writing gift he didn't know he had. Now churches all over the country are using Marty's curriculum. More importantly, the next generation is learning the story of redemption in God's Word.

There are dozens of people, like the Fannons whom you met in the last chapter, who have adopted kids from all over the world. Now these parents are teaching and training their kids and entrusting the gospel to them. I get thrilled just thinking about what that could mean for the spread of the gospel in their generation.

There are men who turned down promotions to make their church and family a priority. There are singles who serve heroically every year at our youth camp. There's the father who taught his kids how to play different instruments so they could help him lead the children's worship time at church. And there are couples who have raised children well and are now helping to shepherd their grandchildren.

A true test of gospel application is seen in succession—in the health of what we leave behind.

I think these folks understand something. A true test of gospel application is seen in succession—in the health of what we leave behind. It's a biblical way to measure success.[2]

If we simply build a church that fragments upon transfer, how does that glorify God or really serve the next generation? It doesn't. Transfer isn't about merely protecting programs or salvaging a legacy. It's about preserving the gospel and passing it on to others. It's about continuing the work of entrusting: "And what you have heard from me in the presence of many witnesses entrust to faithful men who will be able to teach others also" (2 Tim. 2:2).

Covenant Fellowship Church is full of ordinary-but-wonderful people who are passing the gospel baton to the next generation. They're living out the scriptural command to "tell to the coming generation the glorious deeds of the LORD, and his might, and the wonders that he has done" (Ps. 78:4). As a community, they're doing all they can to rescue ambition for their children and grandchildren.

Can you tell I love my church? And I'm not even the senior pastor anymore!

Path Five: Ambition Embraced

That October Sunday would not have happened without an answer to prayer—a man who was called and identified to take my place. Jared Mellinger is that man. He's a good twenty years younger than me. The first time I met him, he was an unconverted thirteen-year-old rebel who had fallen fast asleep in the front row while I preached at the church his father pastored. I was intrigued by his defiant disinterest in what I had to say. I liked him immediately.

Jared was a young man with no discernible ambition save to become an X-Games Rollerblade medalist. But God intervened in Jared's life, capturing his heart and creating an ambition for the kingdom of God. Eventually this ambition focused toward the full-time call of pastoral ministry. After appropriate training, Jared arrived at our church as an intern with lots of smarts but precious little experience. His only goal was to someday be a pastor—wherever somebody would have him. Little did he know what God had in store.

Over time the pastoral team began to see a mix of gifts in this young man that seemed to answer our prayer for my replacement. What we didn't realize was how God was forming an ambition for this very opportunity in Jared himself. Here's how he described it to the church when we announced the transition:

> I definitely didn't come to Covenant Fellowship Church thinking this would happen! The men on the pastoral team know that I have in no way sought this out or put myself forward for this task or suggested that "I'm obviously the man for the job." My résumé is very unimpressive. You have to understand: my idea of a big ambition has always been to simply serve as a pastor in Sovereign Grace Ministries.
>
> All of this is quite humbling and sobering and astonishing to me. I'm being asked to lead a church I did not build, to serve

alongside a team of men whom I did not train, and to speak from a platform I did not create. I'm being called to reap the harvest that others have sown, and celebrate the grace that has been cultivated through decades of labor that my hands have not participated in.

And yet, I want you to know that I do believe that I am called to this task. I believe that God himself has placed a call on my life, a call that has been confirmed by these men, to be the next senior pastor of Covenant Fellowship Church. Therefore, I'm full of faith. I am in no way reluctant to assume this responsibility, but very eager to do so.

I would not be able to assume this responsibility apart from the men who surround me on this team. Were I not surrounded with men who surpass me in wisdom and experience, it would not be wise for me to take on this responsibility, and I would not be in faith for this transition.

However, the primary reason I am in faith for this transition is the faithfulness of God. Ultimately, this transition is about something far greater than any of us—this is about the unrelenting, unstoppable faithfulness of God to his people.

I'm excited about our future together. My ambition is simply to be faithful. My ambition is to lead by example. My ambition is to spend my life preaching Christ and him crucified to you. My ambition is to run the race well and finish well.

I'm aware that one day I will be replaced. In fact, I have already starting praying to this end. Someday I will step out of this role and hand it over to a younger man, and I believe that God will show himself faithful again on that day.

Jared's story is a story of ambition embraced. If you've read this book wondering if it will charge up some malfunctioning ambition circuit in your life, let Jared inspire you. Don't focus on what *you're* to do; focus on what God has done for you. He is faithful, and he'll show his faithfulness to you.

Lead the Way

On the Sunday we announced this transition, I asked my friend Andy Farmer to share some closing thoughts. Andy's the ideal guy for this. He's been a member of this church from the very beginning—just a little longer than me. He has served faithfully with us for a quarter of a century, both as a layman and—for the past eighteen years—as an elder and pastor. Andy has seen it all here. So there was no better man in my mind to offer perspective on what was taking place in this transition than Andy. Let me simply quote what he said as a way to offer a taste of the spiritual satisfaction that comes when ambition finds its God-given fulfillment.

> This transition is about a church that is growing up. My generation started this church, laid its foundations, established its culture, and developed its vision. And we have the potential to turn all that into a monument to the past. The test of a good church is its ability to retain its core biblical values as it passes from one generation to the next.
>
> The test of good church leadership is to entrust what we love to younger men—and let them lead it. That doesn't mean that my generation, and those of you who are older than me, take a backseat to the youngsters. It means we have a grown-up church—each member, regardless of our age, doing what is best to make sure this church stands the test of time and transition.
>
> We're at the moment of decision on that right now. We all feel it. Do we look back and hold onto what had so much meaning for us in the heady days of our youth? Or do we prepare for the future and turn the thing over to leaders who see it with clearer vision than we possess?
>
> This transition will begin to take the church we built and give it to the children we've built it for.
>
> And in my mind, that's holy ground.

As I left the stage that morning and took my place as a member of Covenant Fellowship Church, I had a huge smile on my face. How could I not smile? God bestowed upon me a rare privilege: to identify, train, and install my replacement so I can now serve to make him successful. The proclamation and application of the gospel would continue in strength under Jared's leadership.

As I looked around and took it all in, I silently thanked God that I could be part of a process that began with Christ, continued under Paul, and was entrusted to Timothy, who in turn passed it along to other faithful men who likewise would teach others (2 Tim. 2:2).

This story isn't really about me, or Jared, or Covenant Fellowship

Church. It's about having a definition of gospel success that sparks dreams, not just for ourselves but for our children, grandchildren, and great-grandchildren.

Maybe you're a pastor; maybe you're not (and have no desire to be). But none of us can spend our lives dedicated to God-glorifying work without a plan to entrust it to those who follow us. Godly ambition aims to find faithful people to whom we'll transfer the gospel of Christ, and insist that they do the same. True success means we turn things over to the younger generation in a way that enables them to run stronger and faster, with us cheering them on.

What's Your Story?

That concludes this story, but there's another one opening up for you . . . and for anyone who rescues ambition for the glory of God. Godly ambition is about *your* story—the part yet to be written. The part where God inspires changes in your life today in order to fulfill your story tomorrow.

This book is an impassioned plea. I want to ignite in you the kind of dreams that matter. Not the self-centered kind of dreams, the ambition that uses people and evaluates success only by ascent, that thinks only of what we can see and do. No, I'm talking about the white-hot, courageous, fiercely humble, and humbly fierce ambition that burns to see Christ's name exalted and God's purposes advanced—now and for all time.

We need an ambition that won't rest until more people are reached, more churches planted, more marriages helped, more art created, more enterprises started, more disciples made. We need an ambition that lives joyfully today but wants more *for* God and more *from* God tomorrow.

You may have begun now to consider your story in a different way. You may even sense that God wants you to take specific steps to spend and be spent for his glory. Sensing this is always an exhilarating experience; but the story isn't complete until you *act*. When you set this book down, what steps will you take to begin writing a more God-glorifying future?

Ambition is about *work*—work we want to do for God. But the work we want to do is always built on a work done for us. Godly ambition is gospel ambition. We dream because God rescued our corrupted, selfish ambitions and gave us the capacity to desire, dream, and work for his glory.

So desire great things. Dream big dreams. Get out there and get to work. This world is in need of redeemed people ambitious for God's glory and willing to do something about it.

Why shouldn't that be you?

Afterword:
Why I Wrote This Book

Speaking of ambition . . .

My ambition to write this book took shape over two decades of ministry as I observed a quirky awkwardness among Christians when it came to this topic.

There were the mover-and-shaker types who seemed driven by ambition—perpetually dissatisfied, always hoping the next ministry, job, or status symbol would bring fulfillment. But don't call them ambitious—them's fighting words.

On the other side were the laid-back types—people whose impact never seemed to match their talents and gifts. They knew they had potential, but just never seemed to know what to do with it.

Everybody else just seemed confused. I guess I was one of those. Guys like me wanted to do great things, but we didn't trust our motives, so we were paralyzed because we didn't want to do things for the wrong reason. We live in a kind of guilty frustration, knowing that opportunities abound, but time's running out.

I also discovered that ambition is sort of like sex. It's supposed to be an expression of who we are as human beings, but in many people's experience it turns into, well, guilty frustration. Ambition seems to have an important function, but it gets complicated in real life. Just like sex.

Before I risk overplaying the "ambition like sex" comparison, let me tell you how the two are different. Check your local bookstore. In contrast to sex, which drives more publishing than any topic in the galaxy, there's practically nothing on ambition. Seriously, *nada*. I tried to find it, but it isn't there. You rarely even find the subject mentioned in business books anymore. Sex sells; ambition apologizes for even showing up.

There are, of course, lots of qualities orbiting close to ambition that people don't mind having—competitiveness, assertiveness, and being goal-oriented, to name a few. We admire people who have aspirations in life. Psychological studies list terms like "achievement motivation" and "drive for growth and mastery" as desirable traits in human development. But call somebody ambitious, and you might as well call him or her an amoral, me-centered, backstabbing, social-climbing, power-hungry prima donna. And if you want to stop a prayer meeting cold, just raise your hand and ask folks to pray that you'll be more ambitious in life. I wouldn't recommend this.

Frankly, it would have been a lot easier to write a book called *Ambition Denied* or *How to Succeed without Having to Be Ambitious*. But it's my conviction that ambition shouldn't be left to drown in its bad reputation. There's so much more to ambition than dictators and power-hungry bosses. I trust you've come to the end of this book seeing clearly that ambition is something with a deeply biblical purpose. That's why I think God wants us to join him in this rescue effort. Ambition needs to be set free and put back in play with biblical conviction and gospel clarity.

A Long Struggle

In my research for this book, I found that the struggle with ambition isn't new. Christians have been uncomfortable with it since Bible times. Why? I think it's primarily because in pursuing ambition—as in pursuing sex and money—we inevitably find ourselves wandering into the fields where the world plays. Ambition is active; it throws you into real-time, nitty-gritty interaction with the world around you. That's the way it's always been.

Here's the big picture: ambition is something God intends for good (as we've seen in this book), but it's easily corruptible. In fact, when it's corrupted, it's plutonium, positively glowing with depravity.

That may be why ambition took a mortal blow early in Christian history and never fully recovered. Among the church fathers, ambition was dogged by an assumption of sin. That view later spilled over into Western culture at large, which for centuries was heavily influenced by the church. Ambition became synonymous with the love of earthly position and honor. It meant vainglory, fame-hunting—radioactive stuff.

Understandably, respected voices throughout history decried it.

In his *Confessions*, Augustine called ambition "only a craving for honour and glory."[1] John Calvin termed it "the most slavish of all dispositions."[2] The prevailing sentiment was summed up well by Shakespeare in Wolsey's words to Cromwell in *Henry VIII*: "I charge thee, fling away ambition: By that sin fell the angels."[3]

Despite the bad press, ambition of the worldly kind continued to flourish. It drove men and women to build empires, launch endless rounds of wars, and climb hierarchies of power (even in the church).

Of course, the cleaner form of ambition didn't simply vanish all the while. Sometimes this appropriate ambition was notably evident. Combined with an entrenched religious morality, it sparked needed social advances and government reform—it even aided in the spread of the gospel throughout the world.

In the 1800s, Spurgeon would speak of two kinds of ambition. There was the good kind: "the desire to use one's capacities to the fullest, especially for God's Glory and the good of our fellow creatures." There was also the kind Christianity had always condemned: "that craving for so-called 'glory' which makes a man court the homage of his fellow men, and which will not let him be content unless he is set up on a high pedestal for fools to stare at!"[4]

Spurgeon would also urge believers to pray for "a nobler ambition than that which possesses the common Christian—that you may be found faithful unto God at the last, and may win many crowns for your Lord and Master."[5]

But since Spurgeon's days, the ambition picture has only gotten murkier. It happened as societies and cultures were increasingly redefined and redirected away from a God-centered view of life toward a man-centered perspective and as Scripture was supplanted by human reason as the source of authority.

Ambition points us forward and invites us to aspire to something not yet seen.

More recently, postmodernism has brought a culture-wide denial of any objective truth or authority. And that has rapidly eroded the ground that's needed under ambition. It has practically killed the kind of ambition that promises a hopeful future, since "to be ambitious is to be future-minded."[6] Ambition gets us dreaming about what life might look like if we apply ourselves. It points us forward and invites us to aspire to something not yet seen.

Ultimately only our belief in objective truth—and the hopeful journey toward it—can produce individuals and societies who are courageous, industrious, and enterprising. Without it, we slide into what D. A. Carson calls "a world without heroes."[7] Where objective truth is denied—where there's no meaning, no greater truth, nothing bigger than ourselves—ambition suffocates. Progress and community give way to apathy and self.

Nobody set out to murder ambition. But that was the effect. While many in previous generations were often driven by selfish ambition, today we face a different issue—a generation of young men and women missing the adventure of aspiration. Transcendent vision is lost. The engine of ambition lies silent.

Not long ago I heard a radio interview with a Christian college professor contrasting college students today with those of the past. Decades ago incoming freshmen were marked by their pride—they could (and would) become the leaders, the change agents, the innovators for industry, government, and commerce. Their ideas would influence society and determine the course of civilization. It was class after class of proud, hungry, *ambitious* students.

But over the years the professor detected a distinct shift. Freshmen classes morphed into something else. Gone was the drive to succeed— to aspire to a better life. Replacing it was only the impulse for simple comfort. The professor related how many in this generation have drives and dreams reaching no further than their own ease.[8] There's no cause gripping them, no quest inspiring their imagination. It's not simply the loss of initiative. It's that ambition itself is on life support and gasping for breath.[9]

Colleges aren't the problem; they simply reflect the problem. In a culture fogged over by postmodernism, sadly drive, reason, and argument lie dormant. The future isn't intentionally snuffed out; postmodernism just hangs a "Do Not Disturb" sign over doors of opportunity.

Few risk the hassle of knocking. Fewer still exert the energy to walk expectantly through the door. We go get a latte instead.

Reclaiming the Future

Unknowingly influenced by these cultural trends, the church is undergoing a slow, painless atrophy. The organ of ambition—the God-implanted drive to improve, produce, develop, create, do things—is neglected and well on its way to paralysis. For some Christians, dreams are numbed. For others, there are no dreams; life just happens.

Os Guinness says it this way:

> On the one hand, we are told by a myriad of Christian speakers that we should be thinking about our legacy—the clear knowledge of our contribution after our time on earth. On the other hand, we are told by countless other Christians that ambition is always wrong; synonymous with egotism, it is selfish and quite un-Christian. Both of these positions are wrong. In fact, they are the opposite way around. For as followers of Jesus we can and should be ambitious, but we should never be concerned with our legacies.[10]

To recover this ambition that Guinness says we "can and should" have is the reason I've written this book. I wrote it because I don't want the past robbing us of the future. I don't want the people I love and the people you love to be conformed to the world's way of thinking about today and tomorrow.

As Christians, there's much in the past that we love, but we're also called to the future. It's a future secured by the cross and commissioned by the Savior. A future both given and grabbed, protected and pursued. It's *our* future if we dare to believe God's promises.

That future is too important to put off until tomorrow. We must dream about it today.

I believe God wants ambition back in our understanding of godliness and spiritual health. Sure, let's not fail to evaluate our motives and strive for humility—that's essential. But let's not be paralyzed by self-analysis.

God calls us to "run with endurance the race that is set before us" (Heb. 12:1). He calls us to run it in such a way that we win the prize

(1 Cor. 9:24), to forget what lies behind and strain forward to what lies ahead (Phil. 3:13), to invest our talents wisely (Matt. 25:14–30), and to be a people "zealous for good works" (Titus 2:14). Those are biblical ways to exclaim, "Keep the pistons of ambition pumping for God!"

Let's not just kick-start a conversation. Let's move into the future expecting that God can use us to make a difference.

That's why I wrote this book.

Acknowledgments

Someone once said, "Mountain climbers are roped together to keep the sane ones from going home." I'm no mountaineer, but writing always feels to me like scaling some kind of impassable peak. So here's my strategy: I rope myself to smarter, more grounded minds and scream, "Pull!" until we've finished the ascent. Then we all collapse.

So here are my fellow climbers, and I can't thank God enough that we were roped together on this project.

Andy Farmer, whose imprint on this book mirrors his impact on my life. Yo, A. J., thanks for soaking in the gospel and dripping it everywhere you walk!

Secretary extraordinaire Erin Sutherland. Thanks for your amazing dedication to making me look far better than I am. Not an easy task, as Kimm will attest.

Sarah Lewis, the editorial talent on loan from my friends at Sovereign Grace Ministries. Thanks for finding some clarity in the midst of my authorial chaos.

Rob Flood, who unleashed a few of his many gifts on this project with an impressive zeal, clarity, and ambition to serve. Rob "leaned into" this project in a serious way.

To the pastoral team of Covenant Fellowship Church. Thanks for loving the gospel in a manner so infectious that the church can hardly look away! Only my sons could bump you from the dedication.

C. J. Mahaney, whose vision for this project was displayed by composing the foreword. What an honor to serve you, buddy.

Thanks to Toby Kurth for contributing your scholarship to the Brainerd chapter and to Tim Ashford for helping in the conversion of chapter 10.

Thomas Womack brought some serious game to editing on behalf of Crossway. Whether you like the book or not, you can thank God that Thomas improved it.

Speaking of Crossway, those folks are simply exceptional. Al the signer; Justin the real smart dude; James the market man; Josh on cover duty—quite an impressive team arrayed to serve lowly authors like this one. Thank you.

Let me also offer a quick shout-out to a list of folks who enhanced this project through their ideas and interaction: David Sacks, Matthew Bomberger, Adam Carey, and Tony Reinke. Thank you all.

And finally to my family: Kimm, Tyler, Asa, Shelby, and Alyce (and her brand-new husband, Colin!). You release me so graciously and make coming home so much fun!

Notes

INTRODUCTION: AMBITION'S FACE

1. Near the end of Chapter 29 in Herman Melville's *Billy Budd* (1889).

2. David McCullough, *John Adams* (New York: Simon & Schuster, 2001), 421.

3. Donald Whitney, *Simplify Your Spiritual Life* (Colorado Springs: NavPress, 2003), 132.

CHAPTER ONE: AMBITION CONCEIVED

1. See verses 16, 28 (three times), 41, and 43 (twice).

2. Gerhard Kittel and Gerhard Friedrich, *Theological Dictionary of the New Testament*, ed. Geoffrey W. Bromiley, abridged edition (Grand Rapids: Eerdmans, 1985), 178.

3. Westminster Shorter Catechism, Question 1.

4. Beethoven's improvisation is cited by Edward Said in "Cosmic Ambition," *London Review of Books*, July 19, 2001; http://www.lrb.co.uk/v23/n14/said01_.html.

5. Paul Tripp, *A Quest for More* (Greensboro, NC: New Growth Press, 2007), 18.

6. Nowadays there's a lot of emphasis in Christian circles on the incarnation—how God becoming man should guide our life and service. Some of it is helpful, but some is misdirected, like a ship steaming forward with an uncalibrated compass—plenty of forward momentum, but slightly off course. The incarnation is relevant as good news only when it is understood in light of the saving act of the incarnate Son on the cross. As David Wells observes, "The incarnation was for the atonement," in *The Courage to Be Protestant* (Grand Rapids: Eerdmans, 2008), 197.

7. John Stott, *The Message of Galatians* (Downers Grove, IL: InterVarsity, 1984), 74.

8. Jonathan Edwards, "Zeal an Essential Virtue of a Christian," in *Sermons and Discourses, 1739–1742* (*WJE Online*, vol. 22), ed. Harry S. Stout, 144, the Jonathan Edwards Center at Yale University; http://edwards.yale.edu/archive?path=aHR0cDovL-2Vkd2FyZHMueWFsZS5lZHUvY2dpLWJpbi9uZXdwaGlsby9nZXRvYmplY3QucGw-Gw/Yy4yMToxNi53amVv.

9. Charles Spurgeon, from the sermon "A Good Soldier of Jesus Christ," delivered in London's Metropolitan Tabernacle, Newington. Sermon no. 928 in *Spurgeon's Sermons: The Metropolitan Tabernacle Pulpit*, vol. 16 (1870).

10. Clement of Alexandria, *Exhortation to the Heathen*, Chapter XII, "Exhortation to Abandon Their Old Errors and Listen to the Instructions of Christ."

11. John Stott, *The Message of the Sermon on the Mount* (Downers Grove, IL: InterVarsity, 1993), 160, 172.

12. Henry Scougal, *The Life of God in the Soul of Man* (Harrisonburg, VA: Sprinkle Publications, 1986), 63–64.

CHAPTER TWO: AMBITION CORRUPTED

1. Plutarch, *The Lives of the Noble Grecians and Romans: The Dryden Translation*, in *Great Books of the Western World*, vol. 13 (Chicago: University of Chicago, 1990), 581.

2. Jonathan Edwards, *Charity and Its Fruits*, ed. Tryon Edwards (New York: Robert Carter & Brothers, 1856), 226–227.

3. This statement has been attributed to E. Stanley Jones, twentieth-century missionary to India, and to contemporary English artist David Hockney, among others.

4. Paul Tripp once preached about being self-centered as being Paul-o-centric. Thanks, Paul, for inspiring this illustration and the conviction that comes with it.

5. In the book *When Sinners Say "I Do"* (Walwallopen, PA: Shepherd Press, 2007), I talk about how the gospel includes the doctrine of sin and how this doctrine is essential for understanding ourselves in relation to God and others.

6. David Powlison, "God's Grace and Your Suffering," in *Suffering and the Sovereignty of God*, ed. John Piper and Justin Taylor (Wheaton, IL: Crossway, 2006), 155.

7. Salvador Dalí, quote posted online at "Salvador Dalí Paintings," http://salvadord-alipaintings.blogspot.com.

8. John Chrysostom, "On the Priesthood," quoted in Joost Nixon, "Pastor Traps: Glory, Part 2," *Credenda Agenda*, vol. 13, no. 6:15.

9. Timothy Dwight, "Sermon XXVII: On the Love of Distinction," in *Sermons*, vol. 1 (Edinburgh: Waugh & Innes, 1828), 521.

10. Ibid., 533.

11. Ibid., 523–524.

12. Ibid., 529.

13. Charles Spurgeon, from the sermon "Profit and Loss," delivered on July 6, 1856 in London's Exeter Hall, Strand. Sermon no. 92 in *Spurgeon's Sermons: New Park Street Pulpit*, vol. 2 (1856).

CHAPTER THREE: AMBITION CONVERTED

1. Paul Althaus, *The Theology of Martin Luther* (Minneapolis: Fortress Press, 1966), 213.

2. John Piper, *Counted Righteous in Christ* (Wheaton, IL: Crossway, 2002), 111.

3. "Christ's bearing the penalty of sin is not the whole of his work. Man at creation was put under a law which made life dependent upon obedience. God still holds fallen man to that obedience and, if Jesus was acting for sinners, then obedience was also essential to his work. Thus we read: 'When the fullness of the time was come, God sent forth his Son, born of a woman, born under the law' to redeem us from the law's demands (Matt. 3:13; Gal. 4:4). The sufferings of Calvary were not the beginning of his obedience but its climax: 'He became obedient to death, even the death of the cross' (Phil. 2:8). Christ's obedience is as much related to our justification as is the penalty he bore: 'By the obedience of one shall many be made righteous' (Rom. 5:19)." Iain Murray, *The Old Evangelicalism* (Carlisle, PA: Banner of Truth, 2005), 84.

4. John Piper contends that "active" and "passive" obedience are not always helpful designations: "The word translated 'act of righteousness' in verse 18, ESV (δικαιωματος, *dikaiōmatos*) is used in Romans 8:4 to refer, in the singular, to the entire scope of what the law requires: ' . . . so that the requirement (δικαίωμα) of the Law might be fulfilled in us, who do not walk according to the flesh but according to the Spirit.' This suggests that in Paul's mind the 'one act of righteousness' that resulted in our justification may well refer to the entire obedience of Jesus viewed as a single whole—as one great act of righteousness—rather than any single act he did in life." Piper, *Counted Righteous in Christ*, 12. Piper also cites Jonathan Edwards to punctuate this point: "It is true that Christ willingly undergoing those sufferings which he endured, is a great part of that obedience or righteousness by which we are justified. The sufferings of Christ are respected in the Scripture under a twofold consideration, either merely as his being substituted for us, or put into our stead, in suffering the penalty of the law; and so his sufferings are considered as a satisfaction and propitiation for sin; or as he, in obedience to a law or command of the Father, voluntarily submitted himself to those sufferings, and actively yielded himself up to bear them; and so they are considered as his righteousness, and a part of his active obedience. Christ underwent death in obedience to the command of the Father. . . . And this is part, and indeed the principal part, of the active obedience by which we are justified." Jonathan Edwards, *The Works of Jonathan Edwards*, vol. 1 (Edinburgh: Banner of Truth Trust, 1987), 638–639.

5. Jerry Bridges, *The Gospel for Real Life* (Colorado Springs: NavPress, 2002), 34, emphasis added.

6. John Piper, "J. Gresham Machen's Response to Modernism," 1993 Bethlehem Conference for Pastors (January 26, 1993); http://www.desiringgod.org/ResourceLibrary/Biographies/1464_J_Gresham_Machens_Response_to_Modernism/.

7. "Jesus Paid It All," hymn by Elvina M. Hall, 1865.

8. "The reason why we needed a person of infinite dignity to obey for us, was because of our infinite comparative meanness, who had disobeyed, whereby our disobedience was infinitely aggravated. We needed one the worthiness of whose obedience might be answerable to the unworthiness of our disobedience; and therefore needed one who was as great and worthy as we were unworthy." Jonathan Edwards, "Justification by Faith Alone," in *Sermons and Discourses, 1734–1738 (WJE Online,* vol. 19), ed. M. X. Lesser, 162, from the Jonathan Edwards Center at Yale University; http://edwards.yale.edu/archive?path=aHR0cDovL2Vkd2FyZHMueWFsZS5lZHUvY2dpLWJpbi9uZXdwaGlsby9nZXRvYmplY3QucGw/YzE5OjUuMTguMzIud2plbzo0ODQuODU2NDg3MDk4LjQ5NzExMA==.

9. R. C. Sproul, at the Ligonier Ministries 2008 annual national conference in Orlando, Florida. "Learn to Share the True Gospel of Jesus Christ," Ligonier Ministries; http://www.ligonier.org/blog/2008/06/learn-and-share-the-true-gospel.html

10. See Hebrews 12:7–11.

11. William Carey's original words to this effect are quoted as "Expect great things, attempt great things," from a sermon to a Baptist Association meeting in Northampton, England, on May 30, 1792, as cited by the Center for Study of the Life and Work of William Carey; http://www.wmcarey.edu/carey/expect/expect.htm.

12. B. B. Warfield, *Faith and Life* (Carlisle, PA: Banner of Truth, 1990), 324.

13. Charles Hodge, *Systematic Theology,* vol. 3 (Grand Rapids: Eerdmans, 1946), 144.

CHAPTER FOUR: AMBITION'S AGENDA

1. B. B. Warfield, *Faith and Life* (Carlisle, PA: Banner of Truth, 1990), 289.

2. John Murray, as quoted by Jerry Bridges in *Disciplines of Grace* (Colorado Springs: NavPress, 1994), 74.

3. H. C. G. Moule, *Charles Simeon* (London: Methuen & Co., 1892), 38.

4. Robert Morison, Tamara Erickson, Ken Dychtwald, "Managing Middlescence," *Harvard Business Review* (March 2006), 79.

5. Ibid., 80.

6. Paul Tripp, *Lost in the Middle* (Walwallopen, PA: Shepherd Press, 2004), 139.

CHAPTER FIVE: AMBITION'S CONFIDENCE

1. Tim Stafford, "The Joy of Suffering in Sri Lanka," *Christianity Today* (October 2003), vol. 47, no. 10.

2. Charles Spurgeon, from the sermon "Unbelievers Upbraided," delivered on June 8, 1876 in London's Metropolitan Tabernacle, Newington. Sermon no. 2890 in *Spurgeon's Sermons: The Metropolitan Tabernacle Pulpit,* vol. 50 (1904).

3. John Piper, "Without Faith It Is Impossible to Please God," June 8, 1997, Desiring God Ministries; http://www.desiringgod.org/ResourceLibrary/sermons/bydate/1997/1000_Without_Faith_it_is_Impossible_to_Please_God/.

CHAPTER SIX: AMBITION'S PATH

1. Gene Weingarten, "Pearls before Breakfast," *The Washington Post* (April 10, 2007).

2. Ibid.

3. The Greek word *morphe* "always signifies a form which truly and fully expresses the being which underlies it." James Hope Moulton and George Milligan, *The Vocabulary of the Greek Testament* (Grand Rapids: Eerdmans, 1930), 417.

4. The *New American Standard Bible* translates the first Greek verb in Philippians 2:7 as "emptied Himself."

5. A. W. Tozer, *Of God and Men* (Camp Hill, PA: Christian Publications, 1995), 105–106.

6. Murray J. Harris, *Slave of Christ* (Downers Grove, IL: InterVarsity, 1999), 107.

7. C. S. Lewis, *God in the Dock* (Grand Rapids: Eerdmans, 1994), 55–56.

8. Seneca, *Quaestiones Naturales (Natural Questions)*, 1.17.6, 8, 10; from the John Clarke translation, *Physical Science in the Time of Nero* (London: Macmillan, 1910), 44; http://www.questia.com/PM.qst?a=o&d=94245462.

9. Melody Green, *No Compromise: The Life Story of Keith Green* (Nashville: Thomas Nelson, 2008), 472.

10. Jim Elliot, *The Journals of Jim Elliot*, ed. Elisabeth Elliot (Old Tappan, NJ: Fleming H. Revell, 1978), 174.

11. G. K. Chesterton, from "The Suicide of Thought," chapter 3 in *Orthodoxy* (London: The Bodley Head, 1908).

12. John Stott, *The Message of the Sermon on the Mount* (Downers Grove, IL: InterVarsity, 1993), 172–173.

13. Charles Spurgeon, *The Check Book of the Bank of Faith: Precious Promises for Daily Readings* (Ross-shire, UK: Christian Focus Publications, 1996), 301.

CHAPTER SEVEN: AMBITION'S CONTENTMENT

1. Thomas Watson, *The Art of Divine Contentment* (reprint, London: Religious Tract Society, 1835), 223.

2. Charles Spurgeon, from the sermon "Contentment," delivered on March 25, 1860, in London's New Park Street Chapel, Southwark. Sermon no. 320 in *Spurgeon's Sermons: New Park Street Pulpit*, Vol. 6 (1860).

3. George Marsden, *Jonathan Edwards* (New Haven, CT: Yale University Press, 2004), 361.

4. Charles Spurgeon, "Contentment."

5. U2, "The Fly," *Achtung Baby*, Hansa Ton Studios and Windmill Lane Studios, 1991.

6. Charles Simeon, as quoted by R. Kent Hughes in *Ephesians* (Wheaton, IL: Crossway, 1990), 123.

7. J. I. Packer, *A Passion for Faithfulness* (Wheaton, IL: Crossway, 2000), 206.

8. Sinclair Ferguson, *Let's Study Philippians* (Carlisle, PA: Banner of Truth, 1998), 108.

9. Milton Vincent, *The Gospel Primer* (Bemidji, MN: Focus Publishing, 2008), 47–48.

10. Jeremiah Burroughs, from chapter 2, "The Mystery of Contentment," in *The Jewel of Christian Contentment* (London, 1651).

11. Charles Hodge, *Princeton Sermons*, ed. A. A. Hodge (London: Thomas Nelson, 1879), 106.

12. Sinclair Ferguson, *In Christ Alone* (Orlando, FL: Ligonier Ministries, 2007), 190.

CHAPTER EIGHT: AMBITIOUS FAILURE

1. James Cook, *The Voyages of Captain James Cook* (New York: Walker & Company, 2004), 445.

2. The Yale University editors of the works of Jonathan Edwards note that his *Life of David Brainerd* "was a major impetus and inspiration to the domestic and foreign missionary movement of the late eighteenth and through the nineteenth century." From the Jonathan Edwards Center at Yale University; http://edwards.yale.edu/major-works/life-of-david-brainerd.

3. *The Works of Jonathan Edwards*, vol. 2 (Carlisle, PA: Banner of Truth, 1995), 321.

4. Ibid.

5. Ibid., 335.

6. Ibid., 321.

7. Ibid., 338.

8. Ibid., 335.

9. Ibid., 338.

10. Os Guinness, *Prophetic Untimeliness: A Challenge to the Idol of Relevance* (Grand Rapids: Baker, 2003), 94.

11. Norman Pettit, "Prelude to Mission: Brainerd's Expulsion from Yale," *The New England Quarterly*, vol. 59, no. 1 (March 1986), 48.

12. John Piper, *The Hidden Smile of God* (Wheaton, IL: Crossway, 2001), 129.

13. "Midnight Train to Georgia," lyrics by Jim Weatherly, c. 1972.

14. Arnold A. Dallimore, *George Whitefield: The Life and Times of the Great Evangelist of the 18th Century Revival*, vol. 2 (Carlisle, PA: Banner of Truth, 1980), 418.

15. Edwards's *Works*, vol. 2, 323.

16. Piper, *The Hidden Smile of God*, 129.

17. Edwards's *Works*, vol. 2, 322.

18. Ibid., 338.

19. Ibid., 435.

20. Os Guinness, *Prophetic Untimeliness*, 93.

CHAPTER NINE: AMBITIOUS FOR THE CHURCH

1. Charles Spurgeon from *Spurgeon at His Best*, comp. Joe Carter (Grand Rapids: Baker, 1988), 33.

2. Edmund Clowney, *The Church* (Downers Grove, IL: InterVarsity, 1995), 191.

3. David Wells, *The Courage to Be Protestant* (Grand Rapids: Eerdmans, 2008), 136.

4. Joshua Harris, *Stop Dating the Church!: Fall in Love with the Family of God* (Sisters, OR: Multnomah Books, 2004).

5. Donald Whitney, *Spiritual Disciplines within the Church* (Grand Rapids: Zondervan, 1996), 53.

6. John Piper, *The Hidden Smile of God* (Wheaton, IL: Crossway, 2001), 164.

7. J. Oswald Sanders, *Spiritual Leadership* (Chicago: Moody, 2007), 15.

8. Ellison Research, January 12, 2009; http://www.ellisonresearch.com/releases/Ellison-Research-PR09-1DenomLoyalty.pdf.

9. Wells, *The Courage to Be Protestant*, 33.

10. John Calvin, commentary on Numbers 12:1, as quoted by Wayne Grudem, *Systematic Theology: An Introduction to Biblical Doctrine* (Grand Rapids: Zondervan, 1995), 879.

11. Elton Trueblood, as quoted by William A. Beckham, *The Second Reformation* (Houston: Touch Publications, 1995), 47.

12. As quoted by Iain Murray, *The Forgotten Spurgeon* (Carlisle, PA: Banner of Truth, 1972), 161.

CHAPTER TEN: AMBITIOUS RISK

1. Charles Spurgeon, from the sermon "All of Grace," delivered in London's Metropolitan Tabernacle, Newington. Sermon no. 3479 in *Spurgeon's Sermons: The Metropolitan Tabernacle Pulpit*, vol. 61 (1915).

2. See http://www.sovereigngraceministries.org/Blog/post/Radical-Risk-without-Relocation.aspx.

CHAPTER ELEVEN: AMBITION PAID FORWARD

1. Thomas Watson, *The Godly Man's Picture* (Carlisle, PA: Banner of Truth, 1992), 81.

2. According to Jim Collins, this is also an indicator of whether a business organization can move from good to great. He says that those who lead great companies "want to see

the company even more successful in the next generation, comfortable with the idea that most people won't even know that the roots of that success trace back to their efforts. In contrast, the comparison leaders, concerned more with their own reputation for personal greatness, often failed to set the company up for success in the next generation. After all, what better treatment to your own personal greatness than that the place falls apart after you leave?" Jim Collins, *Good to Great: Why Some Companies Make the Leap . . . and Others Don't* (New York: HarperCollins, 2001), 26.

AFTERWORD

1. Augustine's *Confessions*, book 2, ch. 6.

2. John Calvin, *John*, Vol. II (Grand Rapids: Baker, 2003), 46.

3. Shakespeare, *King Henry VIII*, Act 3, Scene 2.

4. Charles Haddon Spurgeon, from the sermon "Restless! Peaceless!" delivered on May 21, 1876 in London's Metropolitan Tabernacle. Sermon No. 2886 in *Spurgeon's Sermons: The Metropolitan Tabernacle Pulpit*, Vol. 50 (1904), 268.

5. Charles Spurgeon, as quoted by Kerry James Allen, *Exploring the Mind and Heart of the Prince of Preachers* (Oswego, IL: Fox River, 2005), 7, 232.

6. Joseph Epstein, *Ambition: The Secret Passion* (Chicago: Ivan R. Dee, 1980), 5.

7. "Individualism once allied with a societal assumption of objective truth and eternal verities could generate at least some men and women of courage, honor, vision; individualism allied with philosophical pluralism and the scarcely qualified relativism of post-modernity generates 'a world without heroes.'" D. A. Carson, *The Gagging of God* (Grand Rapids: Zondervan, 2002), 49.

8. In a ground-breaking book on educational trends for the twenty-first century, Mark Edmundson observes, "It's a lack of capacity for enthusiasm that defines what I've come to think of as the reigning generational style. Whether the students are sorority/fraternity types, grunge aficionados, piercer/tattooers, black or white, rich or middle class (alas, I teach almost no students from truly poor backgrounds), they are, nearly across the board, very, very, self-contained. On good days, they display a light, appealing glow; on bad days, shuffling disgruntlement. But there's little fire, little passion to be found. . . . This is a culture intensely committed to a laid-back norm." Mark Edmundson, "The Debate: On the Uses of a Liberal Education—As Lite Entertainment for Bored College Students," in *The Social Worlds of Higher Education*, ed. Bernice A. Pescosolido and Ronal Aminzade (Thousand Oaks, CA: Pine Forge Press, 1999), 84–85.

9. Mark Bauerline lists common qualities shared by a growing number of Twixters—young adults between the ages of twenty and thirty: "Instead of seeking out jobs or graduate studies that help them with long-term career plans . . . they pass through a series of service jobs as waiters, clerks, nannies and assistants. Instead of moving into a place of their own, they move back into their house with their parents or into a [place] with several Twixter peers. Instead of forming long term relationships leading to marriage, they engage in serial dating. Despite their circumstances, Twixters aren't marginal youngsters sinking into the underclass. They drift through their twenties stalled at work and saving no money, but they like it that way." *The Dumbest Generation* (New York: Tarcher, 2008), 170.

10. Os Guinness, *Prophetic Untimeliness: A Challenge to the Idol of Relevance* (Grand Rapids: Baker, 2003), 92.